Kin
Kinsella, W. P.
Magic time

$ 19.95

 W9-COI-774

Magic Time

Magic Time

W. P. Kinsella

Voyageur Press

Front cover photo courtesy Minnesota Historical Society. Author photo copyright Bridget Turner Kinsella.

Designed by Andrea Rud
Printed in China

01 02 03 04 05 5 4 3 2 1

Library of Congress Cataloging-in-Publication Data
Kinsella, W. P.
    Magic time / W.P. Kinsella.
      p. cm.
    ISBN 0-89658-575-1 (alk. paper)
    1. Baseball players—Fiction. I. Title.

  PR9199.3.K443 M34 2001
  813'.54—dc21

                          2001026372

Distributed in Canada by Raincoast Books, 9050 Shaughnessy Street, Vancouver, B.C. V6P 6E5

Published by Voyageur Press, Inc.
123 North Second Street, P.O. Box 338, Stillwater, MN 55082 U.S.A.
651-430-2210, fax 651-430-2211
books@voyageurpress.com
www.voyageurpress.com

Educators, fundraisers, premium and gift buyers, publicists, and mar-keting managers: Looking for creative products and new sales ideas? Voyageur Press books are available at special discounts when purchased in quantities, and special editions can be created to your specifications. For details contact the marketing department at 800-888-9653.

Prologue

"Mike, I think I've found you the perfect place to play baseball," my agent said, the line from his office in Los Angeles to my home in a suburb of Chicago as clear as if he was sitting across the kitchen table. My father *is* sitting across the kitchen table, looking expectant. On the first ring, I had reached behind my head and snatched the canary-yellow phone off the hook; it had interrupted our Scrabble game. As I listen, I make a little motion with my thumb and first finger, like a bird feeding. My father smiles.

My agent's name is Justin Birdsong, and we've never met. He signed me because a year ago I looked like a top prospect for the Bigs. It's been a long time since I heard from him. I wasn't picked up in the most recent college draft, but Justin Birdsong said he was impressed with my credentials and would try to find me a job in minor-league baseball.

Not being drafted was a particular disappointment, though not unexpected. I was prepared for the worst, but right to the last moment I had fantasies of the Cubs drafting me onto their Triple A team in Des Moines, or the White Sox announcing that I'd be the new second-base man at their Vancouver Triple A franchise, and that I'd need only a few weeks' seasoning before jumping to the Bigs.

I also dreamed of playing baseball in Japan, though I knew the Japanese usually signed utility outfielders who couldn't quite cut it with a big-league club, and aging power hitters who could no longer get around on the fastball. As the draft continued I shifted my hopes to desperate teams like Oakland, Montreal, or Philadelphia—maybe they would find me a spot, any spot, in their organization. But nothing materialized.

In my junior year at Louisiana State I'd been drafted by the Montreal Expos in the fourth round, and offered an excellent signing bonus, which, after consulting with my dad, I turned down because I wanted to finish my degree in business management, and because we—we being my dad, myself, and my coaches at LSU—felt I needed another year of college experience.

Unfortunately, my final year as an LSU Tiger was one long, downward spiral. My chances of being drafted would have been better if I'd been injured— I would have had something on which to blame my decline. After being a college all-star in my junior year, my average fell from .331 to .270, my stolen bases from forty-five to nineteen, and I was caught stealing nine times. My walks declined twenty-nine percent. My play at second base, which has always been just adequate, remained that way. My promise had been as a high-average lead-off man who could also steal a ton of bases, like Rickey Henderson in his prime.

I don't blame the pros for not drafting me. I have no excuses about my senior year but with that hope that springs eternal in every ballplayer's heart, I feel that with a solid season of minor-league baseball this summer I'll still be young enough for the pros to have another look at me.

After this year's draft, *Baseball America* mentioned that I was the best-looking second-base man not drafted. "In practice, Mike Houle is as good as anyone who's ever played the game. Perhaps with experience he'll get a second look from big-league scouts."

"I can get you a contract with this team in Iowa," Justin Birdsong was saying. "League representative called this morning, one team has openings for several players, but they're especially interested in you. Asked about you specifically. You'll be with a semi-pro club in the Cornbelt League. They claim they play good-quality baseball. Double A quality, they assure me. They also tell me that major-league scouts make regular stops at all the ballparks in the league. You ever heard of the Cornbelt League, Mike?"

"No. Have you?"

"I just thought with it being in the Midwest and all . . ."

"What part of Iowa is it in?"

"East-central, the guy said. He was quite a small-town booster, could get a job as a sideshow barker any time. Gave me a sermonette on the advantages of small-town life. By the time he finished I was homesick for my folks' little clapboard house in Arkansas—for about fifteen seconds until I remembered having to sit in the balcony of the movie theater, and that there were two sets of washrooms and water fountains at the town service stations."

It had never occurred to me that Justin Birdsong was black.

"Anyway, are you interested?"

"Teams in organized baseball aren't exactly burning up the wires to either of us."

"That's the spirit," said Justin. "I'll tell them you accept. They'll wire you your travel money. You're to report to Grand Mound, Iowa, day after tomorrow. You fly into Cedar Rapids and someone will meet you there. By the way, since the Cornbelt League is unaffiliated, all the teams are self-supporting. What will happen is you'll get a base salary, and one of the local merchants will give you a job in the mornings. You'll have your afternoons free to practice and your evenings to play baseball."

The salary he named wasn't enough to pay room and board, and I told him so.

"You get free board, and you room with a local family, so that lowers your overhead considerably."

"Great! I get to live *American Gothic*."

"In case I didn't mention it," Justin Birdsong added, "I only take commission on your baseball salary."

"What kind of morning job?" I asked. "I'm a business major, I don't want to work in a packing plant or a welding shop."

"They were real excited about you being a business major, one of the reasons they asked for you. The local insurance office will pay you to work for them. You'll do fine, Mike. They're go-getters out there, small-town proud, real excited about having you play baseball in Grand Mound."

"It doesn't look as if I have much choice," I said. "I'll be there."

1

Judging Distances

ONE

My father is a remarkable guy. The older I get the more remarkable I find him. He does not look the way most people would imagine a gentle, self-sacrificing father should look. Dad is a large, lumpy-looking man with coarse hair down his arms and across the backs of his hands. His black hair is receding from his wide forehead, and he suffers from perpetual five o'clock shadow. His huge hands are grease-stained and scarred, his brown eyes large and sad, but they sparkle like polished oak when he smiles, a dimple breaking at the right corner of his mouth.

"In baseball you make the same play thousands, even hundreds of thousands of times, Mike—though, like snowflakes, each one is unique. But it's patience and persistence that carry you through. The same patience and persistence won over your mom.

"You must have wondered how an old warthog like me managed to marry such a beautiful girl. When I was young I wasn't handsome, I wasn't rich, I wasn't an athlete, and I wasn't a hoodlum, so if I was gonna convince the girl I'd been in love with since fifth grade to marry me I was gonna have to do it on my own. Gracie only lived a few blocks away and we'd been in the same school all our lives. She considered me a friend, someone who'd always been there—like one of the old buildings downtown.

"Final year of high school, I was already working weekends at the box factory, and your mom worked a four-hour evening shift at the old Woolworth's. Her dad had been injured in a car accident and out of work for months. She was dating a guy named Karl, who was handsome, a fullback on the football team, and had a recklessness about him that caused girls to turn and stare when he walked down the street.

"The one bad thing I knew about Karl was that he was never on time, and for me that was like a pitcher knowing that a batter swings at the curve in the dirt. I showed up at Woolworth's at closing time, and stopped to chat with Gracie as she waited. I said I was on my way home from the box factory, but actually I watched the clock like a hawk and scooted out of the house in time to arrive just as Woolworth's was closing.

"Sometimes Karl was really late, and Gracie would get cold or tired, or both. I never said anything against the guy. I'd run across the street and get us coffee from the all-night diner, and remember to put one sugar and one and a half creams in hers, and I'd try to have a new silly joke to tell her. (Slug jokes were big then. What slug sees out the old year? Father Slime. What's a slug's favorite song? 'As Slime Goes By.')

"I can't tell you how happy I was the night when, after more than a half-hour wait, Gracie said, 'To hell with him. Walk me home, Gil.'

"The next couple of nights he was on time, but it didn't last. This went on for months. One night I got to the store early, and bought a timing chain, car polish, and a fancy gearshift knob for an old car I was trying to get running. When Gracie came out I showed her my purchases and said, 'You know, after you marry me we're gonna have the best maintained car in the neighborhood.' Gracie laughed her merry laugh, but the glance she gave me said it all. Not a month later she came out of the store and said, 'Karl and I aren't going together any more.' By that time I was finished school. A year later we were married.

"You know what I used to like best? After Karl showed up, whether Gracie was walking away with him, or whether she was getting into his old man's car, she always turned and waved to me, and gave me a big smile."

Dad would stop, sometimes there'd be a tear in his eye.

"I miss your mom more than anybody could ever know."

The nail and a half-inch of Dad's right middle finger predeceased him many years ago, slashed off by a saw at the lumberyard where he's been employed all his adult life, working his way up from stacking lumber to feeder in the sawmill to servicing the equipment, to full-fledged maintenance mechanic.

I was in first grade the day Dad lost the tip of his finger. I came home after school to find Dad in the living room rather than Mrs. Schell, who babysat my kid brother Byron and me while Dad was at work. He was sitting in his favorite chair, a leg slung over one arm of it, watching a game show on television, drinking a Tab.

"What are you doing home?" I asked.

"Had a little accident, Mike," Dad said, turning toward me, holding up his hand so I could see his middle finger bandaged in a halo of white gauze, like snow in a coal bin in contrast to the rest of his hairy, grease-stained fingers.

"Had a little run-in with a saw I was repairing. Forgot to unplug it." And he grinned, his face emitting light. "As you can see, I came out on the short end of the run-in, in more ways than one."

As I came closer I saw that there was a bright red spot, like the center of a Japanese flag, on the white gauze at the end of the damaged finger. My stomach lurched like it did when Dad and I went over the top on the carnival ferris wheel. I climbed into his lap and burrowed, trembling, into his warmth, soaking up the comfortable odors of grease, tangy sawdust, and Dad's sweat.

'What's the matter, son?"

"You're not gonna die, are you?"

"Of course not. It takes more than a saw to do in an old warhorse like me. Doc says I'll be back to work in a week. In the meantime, the Cubs are in town, so I'll pick up tickets for you and me. Maybe we'll even take Byron to the Sunday afternoon game, though you have to take your turn ferrying him to the bathroom." Byron was in play school at the time.

I hugged Dad as hard as I could, burying my face in the comfort of his plaid flannel shirt, and held on until my arms hurt.

"You don't have to worry, Mike. Your dad's never gonna leave you." And he rocked me in his arms.

I pulled myself up and kissed his blue-whiskered cheek. Dad always knew the right thing to say. Neither of us mentioned Mom, but we both knew what caused me to get all scared and shaky.

Though I claim to remember my mom, who died when I was four, I think what I remember are Dad's stories of her. What

I remember is sitting on Dad's lap, him holding their wedding picture, an eight-by-ten that still sits on his bedside table, Mom younger than I am now, and beautiful, and Dad telling me about how they began dating, and how thrilled he was when Mom said she'd marry him.

"Look at that, Mike, I look like a gorilla in a tuxedo. What do you suppose your mom ever saw in me?"

Or else he'd hold the family portrait one of those door-to-door photographers took not long after Byron was born. I'm sitting on Dad's knee, dressed in yellow shorts, with a white shirt and yellow bow tie, while Mom is holding Byron wrapped in a blue blanket, all that's visible of him a little pink circle of face. Dad would talk about the day the portrait was taken, how I was so hyper that, though you can't see it in the picture, he had a firm grip on the back of my shorts in order to keep me from leaping off his knee.

"Your mom had just washed your face for the third time since the photographer got there. She wiped it again, tossed the washcloth over her shoulder in the general direction of the kitchen, and said to the photographer, who looked like he'd slept in his car with a bottle of cheap wine, 'Shoot us quick before any more dirt gravitates to that boy's face!'"

Other times we'd look at dog-eared photographs from the chocolate box of photos that always sat on the mantel of the pretend fireplace in the living room. There were pictures of Mom next to a half-washed car; in jeans, shirttails flapping, as she ran laughing from a spray of water. Dad said that photo was taken before they were married, and he was on the other end of the hose. There was a color Polaroid of Mom in a yellow waitress uniform, her name, *Gracie*, in brown lettering above her pocket, her red hair spilling over her shoulders, smiling like she'd just received a ten-dollar tip. Her hair was so pretty in that photograph, and the photo was so clear I could see the freckles on her cheeks and the back of the hand that's visible.

"You boys got the best of both of us," Dad would say, holding up a picture of Mom smiling over a birthday cake flaming with twenty-three candles, Dad behind her chair, crouched in order to get into the picture, grinning like a fool, his fingers in a V above Mom's head, making her look like she has rabbit ears.

"You're both built strong like me, with big bones, but you're good lookin' like your mom."

Byron is stocky, but he has Mom's red hair and green eyes. I'm tall and slim like Mom, but I'm strong-boned and have huge hands like Dad. My hair is reddish-brown, and has a cowlick that refuses to submit to a comb, my eyes a greeny-hazel.

Mom's name before she married Dad was Grace Palichuk. Her grandfather had emigrated from Ukraine to work in the packing plants in Chicago. My grandfather, Dmetro Palichuk, followed in his father's footsteps at the packing plant, but chose an Irish girl to marry, Margaret Emily O'Day, with dark rose-colored hair, green eyes, and freckles.

Our family name is Houle. My father's name is Gilbert. Dad claimed the original Houle was a smuggler and privateer, a crewman on Jean Lafitte's pirate ship.

"Lafitte and his men fought for the Americans in the Battle of New Orleans and were pardoned by President Madison. I saw the pardon, or at least a copy of it, when I was a boy. That original Houle settled on Galveston Island after the Civil War, but who knows how one of his descendants got to Chicago?"

Sometimes Dad tells of a descendant of that first American Houle, a Wells Fargo driver and buffalo hunter in the Dakota Territory, who married a Black Hawk Indian woman (or Nez Percé, depending on his mood) and later became a livestock dealer before being wiped out by the great Chicago fire.

"Your great-grandfather got mistaken for Billy the Kid. This was in some wild Colorado mining town. He was a skinny little guy with a big mustache. The town folks spotted your great-grandfather riding into town, and some young bucks tried to force him into a gunfight. He moved real careful and unbuckled his guns, let them fall to the ground. 'You wouldn't shoot an unarmed man would you?'

"They didn't shoot him, but they flung him in jail and decided to have a public hanging in three days. And it would have gone ahead except the real Billy the Kid rode into town. It was said he had a look about him, a rock hardness, a death-like stare. Nobody tried to provoke *him* into a gunfight. He made it clear he was Billy the Kid, and dared anybody to do anything about it. He even visited your great-grandfather in jail. He laughed when he saw him. 'You look like a gunfighter Ned Buntline might have invented. You don't look nothin' like me.' Billy said.

"'Send this little cowboy on his way,' Billy told the sheriff, and the sheriff did as he was told. It's said your great-grandfather never again wore a gun on his hip, and skedaddled out of Colorado like he was being chased.

"It was one of his boys that got fleeced out of his socks in a gold-stock scam. I did see a photo of him, and he resembled your cousin Verdell in California; you know, a boy so dumb he'd sell his car for gas money."

* * * * *

17

Mom died after being hit by a car right in front of our house. We lived in this quiet, working-class suburb of Chicago, in a wartime house, one of thousands of almost identical box-like structures built right after the Second World War to house returning servicemen and their families. The house was already twenty-five years old when my parents acquired it, just a year before Mom was killed.

Schiffert Box and Lumber, where Dad worked, was an old-fashioned company that had been founded in 1890. They hadn't manufactured wooden boxes since the 1960s, but retained that part of the name. Dad got paid every Friday, in cash. It's only within the last five years that Schiffert has paid by check and at two-week intervals.

Every Saturday morning Mom would do the weekly grocery shopping. On Friday evenings she would circle the loss leaders in each grocery ad or flyer, then we'd tour the supermarkets buying only the items on sale.

I was holding Byron's hand, walking from the house, across the lawn, which Dad kept smooth as a golf green, toward our Ford Maverick, parked at the curb. The car was a shade of gold that Dad laughingly said the used-car salesman had referred to as Freudian Gilt.

The day was hot and breezy, with a few sheep-sized white clouds floating across the sky. Mom was wearing a white dress with red anchors patterned on it, white shoes, and a wide-brimmed straw hat with a red ribbon around the crown. Her family had been over for dinner the previous Sunday and Mom had borrowed some folding chairs from Grandma Palichuk, which we were going to return after shopping.

Mom had the trunk of the car open, had one chair inside and was reaching for a second when a gust of wind whipped her hat off. The hat hit the pavement beside the car, turned on edge, and rolled like a plate into the street. Mom moved instinctively to chase it.

She only took about three steps, the street was narrow and three steps was far enough for her to move right into the path of an oncoming car, driven by George Franklin, who lived only a block down the street. George Franklin didn't even have time to apply the brakes. The car hit Mom, carried her about twenty feet down the street and deposited her on the pavement. I can still hear the sound of her head hitting the street. She died instantly, the doctor who arrived with the ambulance said.

Dad was mowing the back yard with a gas lawnmower, so he didn't know anything unusual was going on. Someone had to go to the back yard and get him. The neighbors didn't think to keep Byron and me away from the scene. I was sobbing because I knew what had happened was not play. Byron and I looked down at Mom, and Byron said, "Mama sleeping?" and through my tears I said, "Yes, Mama's sleeping."

Then a woman in a swirling gray housedress took us each by the hand and hurried us into her house. Even though the doctor pronounced Mom dead at the scene, Dad insisted on riding with the ambulance to the hospital.

Mr. Franklin was not at fault. He wasn't speeding. He was in the correct lane. His car was in good mechanical condition. Between the accident and the funeral, Dad walked us down the block to Mr. Franklin's house. I held onto his right hand, and he carried Byron in the crook of his left arm.

Mr. Franklin was a tall, gaunt man with a hairline that went back like a horseshoe, a crooked nose, and sad blue eyes that protruded slightly.

"I just want you to know I realize what happened was an

accident," Dad said to him. "There was nothing you could do. Gracie should have looked before she ran into the street after her hat. You were just in the wrong place at the wrong time. It could have happened to anyone." Dad held out his hand to Mr. Franklin.

Mr. Franklin's hand was trembling violently as he reached to shake my dad's extended hand. He spoke very softly. He said he hadn't slept since the accident, didn't know if he'd ever sleep again.

"Don't be hard on yourself," Dad said. "It could have been your wife. It could have been me driving home from the hardware store on a Saturday morning."

There was no way Dad could have done more—I don't know if I could be so generous in similar circumstances—but what he did wasn't enough. Mr. Franklin had a nervous breakdown, lost his job as an accountant with the Grain Exchange. He stopped driving. His family left him. He stayed home alone and drank all day. On the first anniversary of my mother's death Mr. Franklin put a gun to his head and ended his pain.

Dad had a married sister in Kansas City; my mother had one in Chicago and one in Milwaukee; and Grandma Palichuk lived only a ten-minute drive from us. Each of them volunteered to take Byron and me, to care for us and to raise us as their own.

And some good cases were made, the best by my dad's sister in Kansas City, my Aunt Noreen, who was married to a lawyer, lived in a five-bedroom house with a swimming pool, had only one child, a girl, Phoebe, and was desperate for a son, but unable to bear any more children. No one considered for a moment that Dad might want to raise his own sons.

But my dad, big awkward rough diamond that he was,

refused all their offers, even ignored Aunt Noreen, who, after being turned down threatened to sue for custody on the grounds that Dad lacked the ability to care for us properly It was about ten years before Dad forgave his sister for that threat. He intended to look after us himself, he said. And when Dad says something, he means it.

It wasn't easy. There were housekeepers, play schools, and day-care centers. There were babysitters who did exactly that—sat—often having friends over who ate everything not locked up. There were housekeepers who drank, who entertained boyfriends, who quit on a moment's notice, stealing whatever they were able to carry.

There were also some wonderful women who tried to be mothers to Byron and me, some hoping Dad would take a fancy to them if they were nice enough to us and kept the house spotless. Others simply loved children. One was a middle-aged lady named Mrs. Watts, a black woman whose family had a cottage on a lake some fifty miles out of Chicago. She took us to the lake for two weeks when I was eight and Byron was six. Dad came down on the weekends and slept in a hammock on the porch of the cabin, and we went fishing and boating and collected rocks and shells. But Mrs. Watts' mother became ill and she had to go look after her instead of us.

It was Dad who enrolled me in Little League, where I immediately showed skill and power beyond my years.

"Did you ever play ball?" I asked him.

"I used to play in a commercial league when I was a teenager. I played third base with all the grace of King Kong. The thing I did best was get hit by the pitcher. The ball didn't hurt so much because I have big bones. I'd lean over the plate and dare the pitcher to hit me, and often enough he would."

We muddled through. By the time I was in first grade I'd mastered the washer and dryer, the vacuum cleaner and the dishwasher. We went to school in clean if unironed clothes. I did the dishes as soon as I got home from school. Byron learned to cook, first out of necessity then for pleasure. I can see him standing on a chair in front of the stove, five years old, frying pork chops, boiling carrots that I had cut up, salting, peppering, shooing me away if I tried to help. We got our share of burns and scrapes and cuts, but we were truly scared only once. When I was six, I reached up and put my finger under the knife as Dad was slicing bread for Sunday morning toast. I still have the scar. There was blood everywhere, and Byron kept a washcloth pressed tightly about my finger as Dad hurried us to Emergency, the cloth turning raspberry colored in spite of the pressure Byron put on it.

"How long will he be on the disabled list?" Dad asked the doctor after he had stitched me up. "This boy's the star of his Little League team and he's only six." I was pale and still snuffling a little. My knees were like water, and I didn't feel the least like a star baseball player.

The hand recovered, and I roared through every league I played in. Our high-school team won twenty-seven games in a row my freshman year and, though we lost in the first round of the Illinois State Championships, I was voted outstanding player.

Afterward, my coach told me a scout from the White Sox had been in the stands for a couple of games.

"Didn't want to put any pressure on you, Son, so I didn't tell you. You've got a big-league future in front of you, or I don't know my baseball players. You've got all the tools. Speed, a strong arm, and a good eye will make up for your lack of power. You're gonna be a great one."

Had he not told me about the scout because he knew I didn't play well under pressure? Or hadn't he noticed? I'd gone 0-5 in our tournament loss, and made an error.

TWO

I was in my second year of high school the day a Cadillac the color of thick, rich cream pulled up in front of Mrs. Grover's Springtime Café and Ice Cream Parlor. Our main street was paved but narrow, with six feet of gravel between the edge of the pavement and the sidewalk. Dust from the gravel whooshed past the car and oozed through the screen door of the café.

Byron and I were seated at a glass-topped table, our feet hooked on the insect-legged chairs. We were sharing a dish of vanilla ice cream, savoring each bite, trying to make it outlast the heat of high July.

It was easy to tell the Cadillac owner was a man who cared about his car. He checked his rear view carefully before opening the driver's door. After he got out—"unwound" would be a better description, for he was six foot five if he was an inch—he closed the door gently but firmly, then wiped something off the side-view mirror with his thumb. On the way around the Caddy, he picked something off the grille and flicked it onto the road.

He took a seat in a corner of the café where he could watch his car and everyone else in the café which was me, Byron, and Mrs. Grover.

The stranger looked to be in his mid-thirties. He had rusty

hair combed into a high pompadour that accentuated his tall front teeth and made his face look longer than it really was. Across his upper lip was a wide coppery-red mustache with the corners turned up and waxed, the kind worn by 1890s baseball players.

Though everything about him was expensive, down to the diamond ring on his left baby finger, he looked like the type who didn't like to conform. I guessed he had grown his hair down past his shoulders when he was a teenager. His hair was now combed back, hiding the top half of his ears and the back of his collar. He was wearing a black suit with fine gray pin-stripes, a white-on-white shirt, and shoes that must have cost three hundred dollars.

"I'd like something tall and cool," he said.

"I have pink lemonade," Mrs. Grover said in a tiny voice that belied her 250 pounds. She had waddled halfway from the counter to his table, but stopped when the stranger spoke.

"I'll have the largest one you've got," he said.

Mrs. Grover delivered the lemonade in a sweaty, opaque glass. He took a long drink, stretched his legs, and looked around the room.

"What do you figure he does?" whispered Byron.

When I didn't answer quickly enough he went on. "A banker, I bet—or an undertaker, maybe."

"He's suntanned," I said, "and bankers have short hair." The big brother pointing out the obvious to the little brother. "And look at his hands."

The knuckles were scarred, the fingers callused.

"What then?"

"Howdy, boys," the stranger said, and raised his glass to us.

His voice was deep and soft.

"Hi," we said.

"I see you're ballplayers." He nodded toward our gloves, which rested on the floor by the chair legs. "Is there much baseball played in these parts?"

The question was like opening a floodgate. We told him about everything from Little League to the high-school team I played for, to the commercial leagues where the little towns, subdivisions, and bedroom communities competed, to the Cubs and White Sox in nearby Chicago.

I ended the baseball lecture saying, "My brother doesn't play much baseball, at least not the way I do. I'm gonna play pro some day."

"How did your team do this year?" he asked me, not in the patronizing way most adults have, but speaking with a genuine interest.

"Well," I said, a little embarrassed, "last year we went to the State Championships, but this season we were two and nineteen. But we're really a lot better ball club than that," I rushed on before he could interrupt—or laugh, as most adults did when I announced our dismal record.

"I keep statistics," I said. "We scored more runs than any team in the league. We're good hitters and average fielders, but we didn't have anyone who could pitch. A bad team gets beat seventeen to two. We'd get beat seventeen to fourteen, nineteen to twelve, eighteen to sixteen."

"They're really good hitters, especially Mike here," Byron broke in. "Mike's gonna make it to the Bigs."

"I practice three hours a day all year round," I said. "I'm a singles hitter. A second-base man. I walk a lot and steal a lot."

"If you're good you'll make it," the stranger said.

"You look like you might be a player yourself," I said.

"I've pitched a few innings in my day," he said, with what I recognized as understatement, and he made his way, in two long strides, to our table.

"The thought struck me that you boys might like another dish of ice cream. Since you're sharing I assume your budget is tight."

"You've had a good thought," said Byron.

"I notice my lemonade cost seventy-five cents, as does a dish of ice cream. I might be willing to make a small wager."

"What kind?" we both asked, staring up at him.

"Well now, I'm willing to bet I can tell you the exact distance in miles between any two major American cities."

"How far is it from Algonquin to Peoria?" Byron asked quickly.

"Algonquin, at least, is not a major American city," said the stranger gently, "but I did notice as I was driving that the distance from DeKalb to Peoria was 118 miles, so you just add the distance from DeKalb to Algonquin." Byron looked disappointed.

"What I had in mind, though, were large cities. Chicago, of course, would qualify, so would Des Moines, St. Louis, Kansas City, New Orleans, Los Angeles, Seattle, Dallas, and, if you insist," and he smiled in a quick and disarming manner at Byron, "I'll throw in Peoria."

"How far from New York to Chicago?" I asked.

"Exactly 809 miles," said the stranger.

"How do we know you're not making that up?" I said.

"A good question. Out in my car I have a road atlas, and inside it is a United States mileage chart. If one of you boys would like to get it . . ."

As he spoke he reached a large hand into a side pocket and withdrew his keys. I had grabbed them and was halfway across the room before Byron could untangle his feet from the chair legs.

The interior of the car was still cool from the air conditioning. It smelled of leather and of lime after-shave. There was nothing in sight except a State Farm road atlas on the front seat. The very neatness of the car told a lot about its owner, I thought: methodical, the type of man who would care about distances.

I carried the atlas into the café, where the stranger was now seated across the table from Byron.

"Let's just check out New York to Chicago," he said. "There's always a chance I'm wrong."

He turned to the United States mileage chart, and all three of us studied it. There were eighty cities listed down the side of the chart, and sixty names across the top. Where the two names intersected on the chart was the mileage between them.

"Yes, sir, 809 miles, just as I said."

The stranger put a big, square fingertip down on the chart at the point where New York and Chicago intersected.

I noticed the stranger had a lantern jaw. He was also more muscular than I would have guessed, his shoulders square as a robot's. His eyes were golden.

I quickly calculated that there were nearly five thousand squares on the mileage chart. He can't know them all, I thought.

"Would either of you care to test me?" he asked, as if reading my mind. He smiled. "By the way, my name's Roger Cash."

"Mike Houle," I said. "And this is my kid brother, Byron."

We were sharing the ice cream because we were saving for a

Cubs' home stand. Dad had promised to take us into the city every night as long as we could afford to buy our own tickets.

"Well . . ."

"No bets, then. Just name some places. Distances are my hobby."

"Omaha and New Orleans," I said.

"Approximately 1,026," Roger Cash replied, after an appropriate pause.

We checked it, and he was right.

"St. Louis to Los Angeles," said Byron.

"Exactly 1,838 miles," said Roger.

Again he was right.

"Milwaukee to Kansas City," I said.

"One thousand, seven hundred and seventy-nine," he replied quickly.

We checked the chart.

"Wrong!" we chorused together. "It's 1,797."

"Doggone," said Roger, grinning sheepishly, "sometimes I tend to reverse numbers. Seeing as how I couldn't do it three times in a row, I'll buy each of you men a dish of ice cream, or something larger if you want. A banana split? You choose."

It wasn't often we could afford top-of-the-line treats. I ordered a banana split with chopped almonds and chocolate sauce on all three scoops. Byron ordered a tall chocolate malt, thick as cement. Roger had another pink lemonade.

"What made you memorize the mileage chart?" I asked between mouthfuls of banana split.

"Nothing made me," said Roger, leaning back and straightening out his legs. "I spend a lot of time traveling, a lot of nights alone in hotel and motel rooms. It passes the time, beats drinking or reading the Gideon Bible.

"I've been known to gamble on my ability to remember mileages," he went on, "and on the outcome of baseball games in which I am the pitcher. I never gamble unless the odds are in my favor, substantially in my favor."

"Do you pitch for anyone in particular?" I asked.

"One season, I tried to take a team barnstorming. But," and he shook his head sadly, "that era is dead and gone. When I was a boy I watched the House of David play, and the Kansas City Monarchs. Must have been about the last season they toured. Costs too much to support a traveling team these days, and with television and all, people don't go out to minor-league parks to see their home team let alone a team of barnstormers.

"No, what I do now is arrange for a pickup team to back me up—play an exhibition game against a well-known local team. . . . Say," he said, as if he had just been struck by a brilliant idea. "Do you suppose you men could round up the rest of your high-school team?"

"Byron's not in high school yet," I said. "But I probably could. Most of the players live close by, a few on farms. Some will be away on vacation, but I think I could round up a full team without too much trouble."

"In that case I think we might be able to arrange a business proposition."

For the next few minutes, Roger Cash outlined his plans, while Byron and I nodded at his every suggestion. It was obvious he had done this thing many times before.

All the time he was talking, I was eyeing the mileage chart, searching for an easily reversible number.

"Have you spotted one that will beat me?" Roger asked suddenly. He had been talking about how many practices our team would need, and the switch in subject caught me by surprise.

"Maybe."

"You want to put some money on it?"

"A dollar." I gulped. I could feel the pace of my heart pick up.

"You're on," he said, turning away from where the chart lay open on the table top. "Name the cities."

"Albuquerque to New York."

Roger laughed. "You picked one of the hardest. A mileage easy to reverse. Now, if I wanted to win your dollar I'd say 1,997." He paused for one beat. I could feel my heart bump, for the number was right.

"But if I wanted to set you up to bet five dollars on the next combination, I'd say 1,979. I might miss the next one, too. People are greedy and like to take money from a stranger. I might even miss a third or fourth time, and I always leave the chart out where a man with a sharp eye can spot an easily reversible number. You men aren't old enough to go to bars, or I'd show you how it really works."

I took out my wallet, opened it up and lifted out a dollar.

"No," said Roger. "I'll chalk that one up to *your* experience. I have a mind for distances. I once read a story about a blind, retarded boy who played the piano like a master. And I heard about another man who can tell you what day of the week any date in history, or future history, was or will be. Myself, I have an idiot's talent for distances."

"What's so great about distances?" asked Byron. "If I was smart I'd choose something else to be an expert on."

"Let me tell you about distances," said Roger, his golden

eyes like coins with black shadows at the center. "Six or eight inches doesn't make any difference, say, between Des Moines and Los Angeles, right?"

We nodded.

"Now suppose you're in bed with your girlfriend."

Roger Cash moved forward, hunching over the table, lowering his voice, because over behind the counter Mrs. Grover was doing her best to hear our conversation. Nothing went on that Mrs. Grover didn't know about. And if there was a shortage of happenings, Mrs. Grover was not above creating some rumors just to get things fermenting.

"Suppose your peter won't do what it's supposed to—you men do know about such things?"

We both nodded eagerly. My experience was more limited than I was willing to admit; but Byron, who was fifteen months younger than me, had always liked girls and girls had always liked him. Though we seldom talked about our sexual adventures, I suspected Byron had more actual experience than I did.

"If your peter won't produce that six or eight inches," our faces were in a tight triangle over the table, and Roger was whispering, "no matter how close you are to pussy, you might as well be 1,709 miles away, which is how far it is from Des Moines to Los Angeles."

Roger laughed, and we joined in, though more from nervousness than appreciation. At the lunch counter, one ear still tipped toward us, Mrs. Grover smiled crossly.

"The distances in baseball are perfect," Roger went on, "ninety feet from base to base, sixty feet six inches from the mound to the plate. Not too far. Not too close. But change any one of them just six or eight inches, the length of your peter, and the whole game's out of kilter."

Byron and I nodded, wide-eyed.

"Well, since you men say you can get me a team, all we have left to do is find ourselves an opponent," said Roger. "Who's the best pitcher in these parts?"

"That would be Silas Erb," I said. "Chucks for First National Bank in the Division One Commercial League."

"Is he crafty or a hardball thrower?"

"Strictly a thrower. Ninety miles an hour straight down the middle, dares anybody to hit it."

"Scratch him. I want a guy who's a curveballer, maybe tries to throw a screwball, has a wicked change."

"That would be McCracken," I said. "McCracken Construction have been Division One Champs two years in a row."

"And he owns the company?"

"His father does."

"Would he be the kind to accept a challenge from an elderly pitcher with a two-and-nineteen high-school team on the field in back of him?"

'Who wouldn't? McCracken thinks he's the sneakiest junkball-pitcher since Hoyt Wilhelm. He throws a knuckle curve."

"If we were to set up this game with McCracken, get posters printed, and talk up this challenge game, what sort of attendance do you think we could expect?"

"People are hungry for good baseball," I said. "I think we could get five or six hundred fans out, maybe more, with people from the new subdivisions."

"Would they pay three dollars a head?"

"No problem."

Roger Cash grinned, the right side of his mouth opening up to show his dice-like teeth. I noticed then, even through the suit, that his right upper arm and shoulder were huge, many inches larger than his left.

THREE

What he proposed to McCracken that night was a winner-take-all game, my high-school team with Roger Cash pitching, against McCracken Construction, Division One Champs and one of the best commercial-league baseball teams in the state.

"I said to him," Roger told us later, "'I'll be happy to cover any wagers you, your teammates, or the good citizens of this area might like to make, all in strictest confidence, of course!'

"'At what odds?' McCracken wanted to know."

Byron and I had waited in the cool interior of the Cadillac, outside McCracken's sprawling ranch-style home, while Roger had done his bargaining and arranging.

"'Even odds,' I said. 'Roger Cash is not greedy.' And you should have seen him smile.

"'I'd like to see you work out,' McCracken said to me.

"'Oh no,' I said. 'The element of surprise is all I've got on my side. I hear tell you played in Triple A for a year, so you're not likely to be surprised by anything an old amateur like me can throw. Myself, I played a dozen games one summer for a Class C team in Greensboro, North Carolina; but they didn't pay me enough to keep my mustache waxed so I moved on. Actually they suggested I move on, but that's another story.' I smiled real friendly at him, and he didn't give me any argument."

Back in front of the Springtime Café and Ice Cream Parlor, after the game was set, Roger led us around to the trunk of the Caddy. Byron and I were on our tiptoes trying to stare over and around him. The trunk was almost as austere as the car interior.

It contained a black valise, very old, almost triangular, with heavy brass latches, and a canvas duffel bag with a pair of worn black baseball cleats tied around its drawstring.

A few garden tools were cast diagonally across the trunk: a rake, a hoe, a small spoon-nosed shovel, all spotless. Built into the depression where the spare wheel would ordinarily have been was a small, black safe, anchored in concrete.

"We're going to need some money to finance this operation," Roger said, and smiled slowly, lines appearing in the deeply tanned skin around his eyes. "I'll have to ask you gentlemen to turn your backs while I operate on Black Betsy here. I'd be obliged if you kept the secret of her existence among the three of us."

Though it wasn't worded as one, Byron and I both recognized that the final statement was a command. We stared up and down the street and studied the windows of the Springtime Café while Roger turned the dial on the safe. It made little buzzy sounds like a bicycle lock.

"You can turn around now," he said finally.

The safe was stuffed with money; from what I could see, mostly hundreds.

The deal Roger proposed was that each of the eight players to back him up was to receive twenty dollars for the game. Byron and I were to be paid extra for distributing posters to the downtown area, and over a thousand handbills to homes in nearby bedroom communities, and on car windshields.

And we were to be paid for selling tickets right up until

game time. Roger also suggested that we arrange to sell hot dogs, soda, and popcorn, since I'd told him no one ever bothered to do that at the local baseball grounds.

He peeled off a few bills from a collar-sized roll, advancing us enough to buy and rent what supplies we needed, and to hire people for the concessions. In return, we were to split the profits with him. For the next few days Byron and I felt like real businessmen, going around town hiring women three times our age to work for us Sunday afternoon.

I suspect it was that experience—Roger letting me see how easy it was to set up a business operation if you had the capital—that decided me on a career in business.

Roger let us know he needed a place to stay. Our only hotel had closed up years before, not long after a Ramada Inn opened in a shopping center a few miles down the highway. I was quick to volunteer our home.

The past few years, since Byron no longer required a babysitter, Dad, Byron, and I had lived harmoniously in what Dad referred to as controlled chaos. We struggled along, sharing the household chores, often on Saturday morning, so that by Friday night we had to push our way into the house, every dish and piece of clothing we owned in need of washing.

"If he can stand it, I guess we can," was how Dad answered my suggestion that Roger move into the spare bedroom until the challenge game.

"If you want to check him out first I can arrange it," I said.

"I've got to start trusting your judgment some time, Son. If this Roger friend of yours steals any of our valuable art work or silverware, you have to pay for it."

Our art work and silverware came from K-Mart.

But Dad was happy to have company, and when Roger arrived carrying only his black valise, Dad was at the door to greet him. Roger accepted a beer and they talked baseball for an hour before Dad headed for bed.

"I need to ask you another favor," Roger said to me the next morning. "I need a place to work out. A private place. I don't want McCracken or any of his spies to see me pitch before game time."

"There's an abandoned ball field behind the factory where Dad works," I said. "They used to have a team in one of the commercial leagues, but they dropped out about five years ago. It's pretty overgrown with weeds, but since all you need is the mound and home plate, I think that can be made playable with an hour's work. And I bet McCracken doesn't even know it exists."

A few minutes with the tools from Roger's trunk cleared away the weeds, and we embedded a new length of two-by-four in the mound to replace one that was squishy and rotten. We dug a small depression and inset two pieces of wood side by side to form a crude plate, after Roger produced a well-worn tape from his duffel bag. I held one end of the tape on the rubber while he measured to the spot where home plate should be.

Roger then dug out his glove and a ball. He gave me the glove and tossed a few practice pitches while I crouched behind the newly installed plate. I guess I was expecting Nolan Ryan. After about fifteen pitches I said, with that terrible candor the young consider honesty, "You're not very good."

"You haven't seen me with an enemy batter at the plate," he replied. "I may not look like much, and I'm no Roger Clemens, but I change speeds and keep the hitters off balance: that's a pitcher's most important function. If they can't time your pitch, even if you're slow as water finding its own level, they can't hit you. Besides, that ain't a catcher's glove, and I wouldn't want to hurt your hand."

"Yeah, right," I said under my breath.

Preparations for the big day kept Byron and me running all week. Tuesday night, my dad, Roger, Byron, and I scouted McCracken Construction during a league game in a neighboring town. McCracken was a stocky, barrel-chested man with dirty blond hair. He pitched a three-hitter. Roger made notes on McCracken, and on the batters he would face.

After the game we discussed strategy.

I had a difficult time tracking down enough players from my high-school team. Several were working shift for the summer and weren't certain they would be available. Some were on vacation. We ended up with a third-string catcher, and I had to recruit Byron to play right field. He was not a total loss as a ball player, but he would rather have charted the game on his computer than play.

"I'm gonna have you lead off," Roger said to me.

I alternated between batting second and seventh most of my high-school career. I showed Roger the statistics I kept on our team's season.

"I prefer being the lead-off man," I said. "How did you know?"

"I know more than you think," said Roger, flashing his disarming grin.

"Look at these stats," I said. "I steal successfully nine out of ten tries. But my high-school coach doesn't play a base-stealing game."

"And you have a high on-base percentage," said Roger. "You walk a lot. Walks are important. You need patience to walk. I need your help here, because I'm going to put my batters up in the order of their patience."

"I don't understand," I said. "McCracken has great control. I went over his stats in back issues of the local paper. They don't always print box scores but the ones I could find show McCracken only walks 2.1 batters per game and averages 6.4 strikeouts."

"You don't miss a trick, do you?" said Roger. "But it's a strategy, trust me." And he smiled once again, his teeth glinting like porcelain.

We had another practice Friday evening. I'm afraid we didn't look very good. Byron reported that someone from McCracken's team was sitting in a pickup truck about three blocks down the street, studying us through binoculars, hoping to get a glimpse of Roger in action.

Roger did not pitch. Our regular pitcher, Dusty Swan, who I had recruited to play third base because our regular third-base man was in California, threw batting practice.

"I want you guys to lay back and wait for the fastball," Roger told us. "McCracken's got a killer curve, a mean slider, a big-league change-up you can break your back on. But his fastball's nothing. He uses it to set up his other pitches. If we can keep from swinging at anything outside the strike zone, he'll give up lots of walks. Then he'll have to throw the fastball and, when he does, we'll hammer it."

Though Roger's strategy went against McCracken's statistics, it was Roger's game, and Roger's money was bet on it.

All that week, in the afternoons, Roger Cash worked out at the abandoned ball field behind the lumberyard. Sometimes I acted as his catcher, but more often he employed Walt Swan, a brother to Dusty. He paid Walt five dollars cash after every workout.

In the evenings, accompanied by his trusty road atlas, he played the mileage game in every bar in the area. Dad heard at work that Roger was picking up several hundred dollars in winnings each night.

"It's also a way for me to become known real quickly," Roger said. "It will help assure a good turnout for the game on Sunday."

By the end of his third evening in town he had a very pretty brunette on his arm. She had a pleasant laugh, a crooked smile, and pale brown, almond-shaped eyes. She was a cocktail waitress at Hot Mama's on the outskirts of town. Her name was Jacqueline, and she spent the rest of the nights that week in Roger's room, except the night before the big game.

"Do you have any objection, Gil," Roger asked my dad our first night at supper, "to my having occasional female company in my room?"

Dad looked up from his chicken-fried steak.

"You can bring a goat to your room as far as I'm concerned," he said, "as long as you're quiet."

FOUR

It was during that week before the challenge game, that I found out a lot about distances myself. Like myself, most of my friends were just discovering girls. Most of our discoveries involved talk. We talked about the mystery of them, we talked about them individually and collectively, often in a disparaging manner learned from older boys at the Springtime Café or the Main Street Pool Hall.

Byron had gone to the movies a number of times with a green-eyed girl named Janice, who wore no lipstick or make-up because her family belonged to a fanatical religious group that thought the end of the world was imminent, and that everyone should be in a natural state when the end came.

"I asked her why she wears clothes," Byron said, after his fourth and final date, "and she said, 'Modesty. The Lord expects modesty from all His creations.'"

It was on that date he discovered the only reason her parents let her go out with him was that he seemed a likely candidate for conversion. That evening, when they arrived back at her house after the show—her father drove them to the movie and picked them up at the Springtime Café afterward—their preacher, Pastor Valentine, and eight members of the congregation were camped in Janice's living room, which, Byron said, was decorated like a church.

Pastor Valentine conducted an impromptu service, and everyone prayed loud and long for Byron's wandering soul. They said many unkind things about the Catholic Church in general and the Pope in particular, having wrongly assumed, I suppose because of our last name being French, that Byron was a practicing Roman Catholic. We had never attended any church, and Dad said our family had had no religious affiliation for at least three generations. "I have no intention of breaking with tradition," Byron said.

Meanwhile I was in love for the first time. Or, more accurately, I had let being in love move from my imagination to real life.

Her name was Julie Dorn, and I had become enamored of her just at the end of the school year. She was a farm girl, almost my height and fifteen pounds heavier. She was clean-up hitter for the high-school girl's softball team, and I liked her because she wasn't a giggler, and always looked me in the eye when we talked. She drove a four-ton grain truck to school.

I was attracted to her straightforwardness, her toughness. Julie tolerated my interest in her, but made it plain she would prefer a more masculine beau, probably one of the broad-shouldered farm boys who knew how to deliver calves and had bronzed arms the size of fence posts. She often teased me about my ignorance of farms and was slightly contemptuous of what she saw as my lack of physical strength. Also, she wasn't impressed by my baseball playing, even though I was often the star of the team both offensively and defensively. She preferred to watch the boys she was attracted to grunt like dinosaurs on the football field. To add to my woes, I didn't drive yet. Julie had been driving farm equipment since she was ten years old.

I called on her about once a week, walking the three miles of narrow pavement that passed her family's farm. She would entertain me in the dark parlor, or we would walk in the sweet dusk, watching fireflies rising, sparkling, dissolving in our path. We even kissed a few times. But Julie never let me forget that my interest in her was much greater than her interest in me.

A couple of days after Roger Cash appeared in town, I walked out to the Dorn farm, arriving at mid afternoon on a high-skied, blazing day. The farm house was tall and sad-looking, badly in need of paint. I knocked at the side door; like farmers everywhere the Dorns did not use their front door. One of Julie's aunts answered, wiping perspiration from her forehead with the back of her hand.

"Julie and her sister are coiling hay in the north pasture," she said.

I could not see into the house because of the thick screen on the door, but from the dark interior came the smell of pork roast, the fumes mouth-watering, almost tangible.

I walked through a grove of trees, enjoying the temporary coolness in the midst of the fiery day. I picked a bluebell, split the bell, and rooted out the teardrop of honey inside.

In a half-swathed field of red clover, Julie and a younger sister were at work with pitchforks, layering the hay into coils, which, when finished, resembled giant beehives.

"You townies don't know how good you've got it," Julie said, driving the tines of her fork into the earth, stilling the vibrating handle, then leaning on it as if it were a tree.

She was flushed and perspiring. Her copper-colored hair spilled over her forehead and was flecked with clover seeds. She wore jeans and a short-sleeved blouse the color of cowslips. The back and underarms of the blouse were soaked dark. She wasn't wearing a bra. I realized that even after my three-mile walk I was still cool. I was wearing a white open-necked shirt and khaki shorts. Even though my hair was lightened by the sun, I had not tanned much. Julie's arms and face were sunblackened, her hair bleached golden in spots.

"Can I help?" I asked, hoping to win favor.

"Sure," Julie said, smiling too knowingly, as if there was some private joke. "Beat it," she said to her sister. The younger girl stabbed her fork into the ground and raced off, happy to be relieved of an unpleasant job.

I have probably never worked as hard as I did in the next fifteen minutes—and accomplished less. I might as well have been trying to coil water with that pitchfork. Julie offered no advice. As I worked, I babbled on about my new friend, Roger Cash, and the upcoming baseball game, mileages, distances, posters, concessions, while accumulating a pitiful pile of clover that bore no resemblance to the waist-high beehives Julie and her sister had created, the hay swirled in circular patterns, the swaths interlocked, impervious to wind, resistant to rain.

While I worked Julie sat in the shade of a dark green coil, smoking, a crockery water jug bathed in condensation beside her.

I finally gave up, red-faced and disheveled.

"It's not as easy as it looks," I said.

Julie grinned with what I hoped was tolerance rather than contempt. "You people in town live so far away," she said, her tone still not definable.

"It's only three miles," I said stupidly.

Julie took a final drag on her cigarette and crushed it out on the earth beside her. She looked at me with a close-lipped smile.

"At least you tried," she said, and leaned over so her head rested on my shoulder.

We kissed, both our faces damp from the heat of the day. The smell of freshly cut clover was overpowering. Julie slid closer to me, crossed one of my bare legs with one of her denim ones. She radiated heat. Her breasts burned against my chest as we embraced, only two thin layers of cloth separating us.

Her tongue was deep in my mouth, her large right hand hard to my left shoulder. Before I realized it she was forcing me down on my back, pushing me deep into the sweet clover. I didn't mind that she was stronger; there was nothing I could do about it. It even excited me. I ran my free hand down the thigh of her jeans, let it find its way between her legs.

We stopped kissing and gasped for breath.

"I bet I could take you," Julie said into my neck, and I knew by her tone that she meant in physical strength.

"You probably could," I said, gasping for air. "What does it matter? You work hard, have all your life. I don't."

Suddenly, Julie forced my head deep into the hay. All the sexuality of the previous moment was gone. This was a contest. Julie's hands were on my shoulders, her right leg between my thighs; she held my back down flat on the stubbly earth.

I had no experience roughhousing with girls.

My worst fear, almost certainly a truth, was that Julie would care about being able to out-wrestle me. How hard should I defend myself? If I concentrated on one of her arms, got a solid lock on it . . . but Julie was sitting on my chest. My shoulders were pinned to the earth, and my head partially covered with clover, the tiny red seeds filling my eyes and mouth, spilling down my neck.

I bucked ineffectually a few times.

"Okay, you've proved your point," I said.

Julie scrambled to her feet. I stood and brushed the clover seeds from my face and shirt front. I wanted to reverse time. I wanted the scent, the taste of Julie; I wanted to be inside her mouth, to feel the heat of her breasts burning against me.

But what I read in her eyes was that I was never to be forgiven for my weakness. I was walking toward her with the idea of taking her in my arms anyway, in spite of the coldness in her eyes, when her kid sister reappeared.

"We've got to get back to work," said Julie.

"I'll come by again," I said. Julie didn't reply.

But as I walked slowly back toward town, swinging my shirt in my right hand, the sun burning my back, I knew I wouldn't.

FIVE

Saturday night, Roger went to bed about ten o'clock. Alone.

"Got to rest the old soupbone," he said, as he headed up the stairs, flexing his huge pitching arm.

I went to bed shortly after, but I couldn't sleep. My mind was too full of the game the next day, my thoughts as much on the operation of the concessions as on baseball.

Eventually I dozed fitfully, but late in the night I woke with a start, surprised to hear the stairs creaking. I stretched out my arm and let the moonlight slanting through the window touch the face of my watch. Three A.M. I went to the window. I heard keys jingle in the darkness, watched as Roger opened the trunk of the Caddy and stealthily extracted the garden tools, hoisted them to his shoulder, and set off down the fragrant, moonstruck street.

About four-fifteen, just as the first blue-orange tinge appeared on the horizon, Roger returned, replaced the tools, and re-entered the house.

By game time we had sold 511 tickets. I left a woman named Margie Smood at the ticket table to sell to latecomers until the fifth inning. The concessions were booming, and the air was alive with the smell of frying onions, hot dogs, and popcorn. There was no fence around the local ball field, so, at Roger's suggestion, Byron and I constructed a funnel-like gate, made of pickets joined by flame-orange surveyor's tape. People were generally honest; only a few school kids and a handful of adults skirted the ticket line.

Our players were all nervous as we warmed up along first base. One thing I'd neglected to tell Roger was that our high-school team had never been able to afford uniforms—although the football team had trucks full of equipment—so we wore whatever we could scrounge: anything from jeans, T-shirts, and sneakers to a full Detroit Tigers uniform worn by Lindy Travis, who was a cousin several times removed of Detroit pitcher Virgil Trucks.

Along third, McCracken Construction, in black uniforms with gold numbers on their chests and their names in gold letters on their backs, snapped balls back and forth with authority. Baseballs smacking into gloves sounded like balloons breaking.

"Where are the gate receipts?" Roger asked me.

"In a box under the ticket table. You don't need to worry. Margie Smood's honest."

"Go get them. Just leave her enough to change a twenty."

"But . . ."

"I've got to get down some more bets."

"What if we lose?"

"Never in doubt, Mike. Never in doubt."

While six members of the Franklin Pierce High School Music Makers Marching Band, in beautiful red uniforms with gold buttons and epaulets, were assassinating the national anthem, Roger carried the money around to a conference with McCracken and his teammates.

The mayor, a small man with white hair and a rodent face, wearing an American Legion beret, was seated in the front row, directly behind home plate, and he had apparently agreed to hold the bets. By game time there were bags and boxes, envelopes and cartons piled at his feet. As near as I could estimate, Roger must have had upwards of ten thousand dollars riding on the game, perhaps as much as twenty thousand, most of it covered by McCracken and his team.

Roger and McCracken talked animatedly for several minutes. Finally McCracken went to his equipment bag and counted out more money; he also signed something that Roger proffered. Roger dug into the back pocket of his uniform and produced the keys to his Caddy. He held them up, let the sun play on them, then dropped them in a box with the money and the paper McCracken had signed. The box was deposited at the feet of the mayor.

McCracken appeared uncomfortable as he warmed up on the mound. One of the concessions Roger offered, even though we were playing on our home field, was to allow McCracken Construction to be home team.

McCracken pawed the dirt and stalked around the rubber. After the umpire called "Play Ball!" his first three pitches were low, one bouncing right on the plate. The fourth pitch McCracken threw was a fastball, right down the heart of the plate, for a strike. I was tempted to hammer it, but held back, telling myself, a walk is as good as a single. McCracken was in trouble, I wasn't, and he walked me with another low pitch. He walked Lindy Travis on five pitches. He walked Gussy Pulvermacher on four. As I moved to third I watched Roger whispering to our clean-up hitter, Dave Urbanski, his heavy right arm clamped on Dave's shoulder.

The first pitch was low. The second broke in the dirt.

McCracken kicked furiously at the mound. I could almost see Dave Urbanski's confidence building as he waited. The fastball came. He drove it into the gap in left-centre for a stand-up double. Three of us scored, as Roger, leaping wildly in the third-base coach's box, waved us in with a windmilling motion.

McCracken was rattled now. It didn't help that the crowd was solidly behind us. Here was a high-school team coming off a two-and-nineteen season, going against a crack amateur team who were state finalists.

Our next batter walked on four pitches. Then McCracken settled in with his fastball and struck out the sixth batter, and Byron, who was seventh. The catcher hammered the first pitch about five hundred feet, nearly to the back yards of the closest housing complex. Fortunately for McCracken, the ball was foul. He reverted to his off-speed pitches and walked the catcher.

Roger Cash stepped into the batter's box. He had confided to me that if he kept a record, his lifetime batting average would be below .100. But he looked formidable in his snow-white uniform with CASH in maroon letters and the large numbers 00 in the middle of his back. The front of his uniform had only crossed baseball bats on it. He held the bat straight up and down and waggled it purposefully.

"Throw your fastball and I'll put it in somebody's back yard," yelled Roger, and curled his lip at McCracken.

The first pitch was a curve in the dirt, followed by a change-up low, another curve at the ankles, and something that may have been a screwball that hit two feet in front of the plate. Roger trotted to first. A fourth run scored, and the bases were still loaded.

On the first pitch to me McCracken came right down the

middle with his fastball. I got part of it with the end of the bat, a dying quail just beyond the second-base man's reach. Runs five and six scored. Lindy Travis ended the inning.

McCracken's team tried to get all six runs back in the bottom of the first. They went out one-two-three.

I bounced around at second base, feeling as though I had insects crawling all over my body I wanted the ball to be hit to me. I dreaded the ball being hit to me.

McCracken walked the first batter in the second inning, but that was it. His curve started snapping over the plate at the last second, pitches that had been breaking into the dirt now crossed the plate as strikes at the knees.

We led 6-0 after three innings. But McCracken Construction got a run in the fourth, one in the fifth when Byron dropped a fly ball with two out, and two in the sixth with a single and a long home run by McCracken himself.

I managed to hit another Texas League single, but grounded into an inning-ending double play in the sixth.

McCracken and his team were at last catching on that Roger was little more than a journeyman pitcher with a lot of guile. He had a screwball that floated up to the plate like a powder puff, only to break in on the batter's hands at the last instant, usually resulting in a polite pop-up to the pitcher or shortstop. His fastball was nothing, and, knowing that, he usually threw it out of the strike zone. But his change-up was a beauty, like carrying the ball to the plate. Roger's pitching motion never changed an iota; a hitter would be finished his swing and on his way to the bench, shaking his head, by the time the ball reached the catcher.

The seventh went scoreless.

49

We got a run in the eighth on a double and a single, but McCracken's team got two in the bottom, aided again by Byron's misjudgment of a fly ball.

It was obvious that Roger was tired. His face was streaked with sweat and grime, he took off his cap after almost every pitch. To compound matters, we went out on four pitches in the top of the ninth, allowing Roger only about two minutes' rest.

With our team leading 7-6, the first batter in the last of the ninth hit a clean single up the middle. The next sacrificed him to second. (I managed to cover first on the sacrifice—my greatest fear was that I would botch that play.) The third batter swung very late on a change-up and sent the ball like a bullet just to the inside of first. Lindy Travis lunged for the ball and, by accident, it ended up in his glove. He threw from a sitting position to Roger, covering the base, for the second out. The base runner advanced to third.

McCracken was at the plate. As he dug in he sent a steady stream of words toward the mound. Though I couldn't hear, I knew he was baiting Roger. Well, if we lost, there would at least be enough profits from the concessions to pay my employees off and buy Roger a bus ticket for somewhere not too far away. All I hoped was that the ball wouldn't be hit to me.

McCracken, even though he was right-handed, hammered one down the right-field line on a 2-2 count. Byron actually ran in a step or two before he judged it properly; then he ran frantically down the line, his back to the plate. The ball nearly hit him on the head as it plunked onto the soft grass a foot outside the foul line.

Roger delivered a fastball in the strike zone.

It was, of course, the last pitch McCracken was expecting.

Roger had thrown nothing but junk the whole game, using his fastball only as a set-up pitch, always, like McCracken, throwing it out of the strike zone.

McCracken swung just late enough to send a gentle fly to right-center. The center fielder waved Byron off and clasped the ball for the final out.

At our bench Roger wiped his face and hair with a towel.

"You get the rest of the gate receipts and the concession money," he said. "One of McCracken's men will count it with you."

"You didn't bet against us, did you?"

"Of course not. I bet it all on us. Which, incidentally, will increase your profits considerably. Even after I take my percentage."

"What if we'd lost?"

"It wouldn't be the first time I've left a town on foot with people throwing things at me."

Roger collected his winnings from the mayor, and stuffed the envelopes and stacks of bills into his equipment bag. He settled his debts, then bought the entire team supper, plus unlimited ice cream, at the Springtime Café. He tipped Mrs. Grover twenty dollars.

Later, while Byron and I again turned our backs, he opened the safe and stuffed it full of bills.

"I'll be on the road before daylight," he said. He gave Byron and me an extra twenty each. At bedtime we said our goodbyes.

Though I was dead tired, I forced myself to only half sleep; I jumped awake every time the old house creaked in the night, and I was up and at the window as soon as I heard Roger's step on the stairs.

As I suspected, he did not leave immediately, but took the gardening tools from the trunk and hoisted them to his shoulder, careful not to let them rattle. There had been a heavy thunderstorm about ten o'clock and the air was pure and sweet as spring water.

I was waiting by the Caddy when Roger returned, clothes soiled, his shoes ruined by mud.

"You been in a fight, or what?"

"I suspect you know where I've been," he said, keeping his voice low. He deposited the tools into the trunk.

"I know a little about distances," I said.

"When did you suspect?"

"I measured your practice field out by the lumberyard. Sixty-one feet from the rubber to the plate. No wonder your arm's big as a telephone pole."

"You figure on telling McCracken?"

"No."

"Don't lie for me. Do what you have to do, it's okay. Just wait until morning. Also, remember that cheating is making your opponent do something you don't have to do. We both pitched from the same distance. It was just that I'm used to that distance, and it took him a while to adjust."

"I'm not going to turn you in," I said.

Roger picked a chunk of mud off one of the tools and threw it on the street. He began to fiddle with the combination of the safe.

"I'm not planning on blackmail."

"I appreciate talent when I see it. I've been working this scam for ten years. I've lost an occasional game, but no one's ever cottoned onto my edge. I must be getting careless."

52

He took about an inch of bills off the top of one of the piles and handed them to me.

"You really don't need to. Money can't buy what I want."

"Which is?"

"I want this girl to like me just the way I am."

"No, money can't do that. But it'll buy a hell of a lot of ice cream, and pay your college tuition for a semester or two." His face broke into that grin that could charm a bone from a hungry dog.

"It's all a matter of distances," Roger said from inside the Caddy. The sun was about to rise. The oranges and pinks of the sky touched the shimmering surface of the white Cadillac. "Chicago to Memphis is 537 miles. I'll have a late breakfast at Perkins' Cake and Steak on Elvis Presley Boulevard."

Roger smiled again, reached his right hand up and out the window to shake my hand.

"Maybe we'll run into each other again, Mike. Be cool. Life's all a matter of distances. Make them work for you."

The window purred up and the car eased away, gravel crunching under the wide tires.

One Road Runs Straight

SIX

My dad must have said it a thousand times. "For a lead-off batter, a walk is as good as a hit. A walk and a stolen base is as good as a double." I can still hear those words echoing in my eight-year-old ears. It didn't matter that I was never a power hitter, as long as I learned the strike zone, which I did.

I learned to bunt, both for a base hit, and in order to sacrifice a runner along. The hardest thing, when I was a kid, was to hit the ball on the ground up the middle. The assumption was that just making contact would earn me a certain number of base hits, and I was so fast I was almost impossible to double up on a ground ball. But, oh how hard that was to do, for every kid has fantasies of blasting the ball out of the park, of hitting a blue darter like a lightening bolt off the outfield fence.

The only time I tried to hit the ball in the air was when a sacrifice fly was called for. I never tried for home runs or extra base hits, controlling my desire to be a hero in return for making a solid contribution.

In the evenings Dad and I would practice in the back yard. Dad would lay down a towel, white as a patch of snow, up the third-base line where a perfect bunt would come to rest, good not only for a sacrifice but often a base hit. Dad would pitch to me while I practiced bunting.

"Pretend the towel is the mother and the ball is the baby, and it's your job to reunite the two," Dad would shout.

Other times he'd yell, "Suicide squeeze!" and drill in a high hard one that I was somehow supposed to lay down.

A hundred pitches minimum every evening, at ever-increasing speed, while I tried to get the ball down in the dirt so it would end up on the towel, while I pictured myself streaking safely across first, the runner in front of me perhaps taking an extra base when the hurried throw to first went wild.

Then there'd be another hundred pitches while I tried to rap the ball straight up the middle on the ground, controlling my urge to belt the ball about four hundred feet, because Dad's pitches looked like white balloons floating toward me.

"Take the sure thing," he'd say. "Don't try to be a hero, hit the ball on the ground for a single. You've only got warning-track power at best, so don't waste your life hitting routine flies to the outfield."

Following that we'd take a break for orange juice or lemonade. Then there'd be another hundred pitches, which I practiced hitting to the right side, behind the runner, trying for a base hit, but willing to give myself up in order to advance the base runner.

"The three-four-five men are the power hitters," Dad always said. "Let them do their job. Your only worry is to get on base or, if you can't, at least advance the runners."

I don't think Dad ever expected too much of me. He never let on that he was disappointed when I didn't perform well, even when I was downright awful. He wasn't one of those sports fathers who got red in the face and screamed like a college basketball coach when his son made a mistake. The endless hitting and fielding practice was my idea. I imagine Dad would have been happier curled up in front of the TV after a hard day at the lumberyard; but when I came along, bat and ball in hand, to drag him out of his armchair, he never complained.

No, I'm the one who has always expected too much of myself. I think it came from recognizing early on how much Dad had sacrificed for Byron and me. I wanted to please him, maybe too much. But I try to avoid that psychological kind of thinking. I've seen too many young hitters lose their careers because they tried to analyze why they were hitting home runs.

Until I went away to LSU on my baseball scholarship, I don't think Dad ever missed a single game. It's a good thing Byron wasn't into organized sports, I don't know how Dad could have kept up with us. Byron discovered computers when he was in first grade, and his fate was sealed.

Dad would keep both hitting and fielding charts on me. He'd sit behind home plate and he'd chart every pitch I swung at, marking down whether it was a ball or a strike, high or low, inside or outside, a fastball, curve, slider, or change-up, marking where I hit the ball, and, if I made an out, where I *should* have hit the ball.

He did the same when I was playing defense, keeping records of where I was positioned on the field, where the ball was hit, how far to the right or left I went for the ball, how well I turned the double play, whether tossing to the shortstop or receiving the ball and turning the pivot, leaping like a ballet dancer over the sliding runner. Dad even offered to pay for ballet lessons if I thought they would improve my fielding. I decided not to, which I now believe was a mistake.

After every game, like bridge players, we'd sit at the kitchen table, replaying every inning, rehashing every play, looking for ways I could improve, striving for ways I could develop an edge.

I had scholarship offers from seven universities, but, ever-vigilant to the possibility that a major-league career might elude me because of injury or such caprice, I chose Louisiana State, the school that appeared to have the best business faculty as well as an A-1 baseball program.

The day I arrived, an assistant coach, a swath of black hair painted across his forehead like a crow's wing, took me aside.

"Mike, y'all play a good second base for us, and everything else will take care of itself. We'll find courses y'all'll be able to pass while giving your time to playing baseball."

"In other words, athletes don't have to take courses that might lower their grade-point average."

"Just trust me. Let me pick your courses," the coach said. "I been looking at the schedule y'all set for yourself, and, well, there's courses there that are downright *difficult*. Statistics, economics, political science, psychology—well, you were a bright student in high school, but you'd have to spend hours and hours studying every week, just to squeeze through. You might not be able to give enough time to baseball."

I stuck to my guns and took the courses I wanted to take, but I was one of the only ballplayers to do so. All the scholarship players seemed to think they were going to be in the Bigs, though it was easy to see most of them didn't stand a chance. At this moment there are four of my LSU Tiger teammates playing in Double and Triple A. Maybe two will make the Bigs. My guess is that only one will stick.

And then there's me. I keep telling myself I'm different—one good summer and I'll catch the eye of a big-league scout, get another chance.

I've always been pretty astute about my baseball abilities. More astute than any of my coaches, even my dad. It came upon me like a revelation when I was about seven years old that I had more ability at hitting, fielding, and throwing than other kids my age. It wasn't long until I decided, that if I did each of those things perfectly, within the range of my abilities, I had a good chance to play professionally.

I had to use every ounce of ability, use it carefully, deliberately, and intelligently. If I worked harder and smarter than anyone else then I'd make it.

And that approach worked.

"You're the most disciplined player for your age I've ever seen," my hitting coach at LSU said to me during my freshman year.

And I probably was.

Until my senior year at LSU.

Ever since my freshman year in high school, I've analyzed how I have performed at the plate, especially how I hit when my team was ahead compared to how I hit when we were behind. I discovered things that I didn't like one bit, things I never discussed even with my dad, and things I hoped my coaches wouldn't notice.

Though my batting average has always been high, I have

been inclined to hit when it didn't count for much. My batting average in extra innings, allowing that all innings from the ninth on are likely to be scoreless, was abysmal. My batting average dived when we played contending teams. I was hell on wheels against small colleges, but when Stanford or Oklahoma or Texas showed up, my bat became spaghetti, and, in the field, I crumpled like a used tissue.

I just didn't come through in the clutch. As the lead-off hitter I wasn't expected to be a star, but even when I was playing well, I felt like a fraud. All through high school and college, I would accept congratulations for a well-played game, then go home and enter my statistics into my computer, and come up a loser again and again.

Now, I'm packing for my first venture into semi-pro baseball. I should be leaping up and down with excitement. But if everything is so damn good, how come my stomach feels like I swallowed a hand grenade? I haven't seen my teammates in Grand Mound, and already I'm worried I won't measure up. Maybe it has something to do with losing my mother? I'm always worried about losing what I have. I sweated and bled over exams. I know if I was promoted to the Bigs and became a starter I'd worry constantly about maintaining my position. I'd be staring over my shoulder like a shoplifter wondering what new infield phenom was about to displace me. I'm always afraid someone is going to take away everything that I have.

Worry, thy name is Mike Houle.

SEVEN

At the Cedar Rapids airport I was met by a large, hearty man named Emmett Powell. The weather was hot, the humidity very high for so early in the season. Powell was in shirtsleeves, his grey suitcoat slung casually over his arm. He might have been an athlete when he was in high school, I decided. In fact he looked a little like some of the retired baseball players you see interviewed on television before old-timers' games. His thinning hair was combed straight back off a high, ruddy forehead; his belly swelled comfortably over his belt.

I'd looked up Grand Mound, Iowa, in Dad's coverless Rand McNally road atlas that must have been nearly as old as me. Grand Mound *was* in northeastern Iowa, and it showed a population of fifteen hundred. That was it. At the library, I couldn't find any mention of the Cornbelt League. I even called a sportswriter with the *Chicago Tribune*, a relative of a friend of a friend.

"There are all kinds of unaffiliated amateur and semi-pro leagues in rural areas all over America, especially in the Midwest and South. Get yourself local newspapers, usually they're weeklies—they'll give those amateur leagues some kind of coverage," the sportswriter told me.

But by that time I was due to fly out of Chicago, headed, as my brother Byron said, for darkest Iowa.

Emmett Powell must have seen a picture of me, because there were several young men of college age getting off the Ozark Air Lines flight in Cedar Rapids, but he headed directly for me.

"Welcome to Iowa, Mike," he said, pumping my hand. "I'm sure you're gonna enjoy your summer in Grand Mound. And, no, before you ask, the town wasn't named for a pitching mound, though a long time ago there was a town down Iowa City way called Big Inning, and *it* was named because of baseball."

We moved the length of the small airport to the baggage carousel.

"You ever lived in a small town, Mike?"

"Yes and no. The town where I was raised is now connected right up to Chicago, and Baton Rouge, where I went to LSU, is smaller than Chicago, but no small town."

"You're in for quite an experience then. Small-town living is heaven on earth, Mike."

I had the feeling he was about launch into a sermon describing the benefits of small-town living, as Justin Birdsong said he had done, but just then my suitcase and equipment bag came gliding along the conveyor belt.

Emmett insisted on carrying my suitcase, a very elderly one with brass-colored corners, trussed up with two black leather straps. As we were leaving the airport I noticed three people, a middle-aged couple and a dark-eyed girl of about seventeen, who seemed to be staring intently at me, as if I were a celebrity they were afraid to approach. I even got the impression they were talking about me. I remembered they had been standing next to Emmett and me in the baggage area. The girl had dark hair and dusky rose cheeks. I certainly didn't mind if *she* wanted to look at me.

I checked my fly. It was not open.

"Do I look odd or something?" I asked Emmett. "Is there something wrong with the way I'm dressed?"

"Of course not," said Emmett. "Why do you ask?"

"Those people we just passed, they were watching me, and I know it sounds odd, but I think they were talking about me."

Emmett glanced over his shoulder, frowned slightly, "Actually it would be me they were looking at. They look familiar, although I can't quite put a name to them—probably customers of mine."

"That's good," I said. But when I glanced over my shoulder as we crossed the circular driveway toward the parking lot, they were still staring at us and pointing.

When we reached Emmett's car, a maroon-colored, top-of-the-line Buick, I was surprised to find there were people in the back seat. In fact, Emmett's whole family was in the car.

"This is my wife Marge, my daughter Tracy Ellen, and the dog there is Sarge—he hates to see us go anywhere and not take him along," Emmett said.

Sarge was a docile-looking brown-and-white spaniel with ears big as pot holders, sitting between Marge, a pleasant-looking woman with pink cheeks and a ready, motherly smile, and Tracy Ellen, who was as blonde and pretty as if she had just stepped out of a 1970s television sitcom. Glancing at Tracy Ellen, I was reminded of playing baseball in Salt Lake City, against Brigham Young University, where the Mormon girls all looked like Tracy Ellen, pretty, freshly scrubbed, glazed with wholesomeness. I wondered for an instant if I might be falling into a nest of religious fanatics.

"You'll be boarding with us this summer," Emmett said, as he eased, the Buick out onto the highway. "In a small town like Grand Mound there's a lot of competition to see who gets to house the new ballplayers. Competition among families with marriageable daughters gets downright fierce," and he chuckled good-naturedly.

I watched as he stared into the rearview mirror until his

eyes met those of Tracy Ellen.

"Oh, Dad," said Tracy Ellen, exasperation in her voice. Her hair was a pale, creamy blonde and she had a few freckles across the bridge of her nose.

"Emmett, you behave yourself," said Marge. "Don't you frighten this boy away before we even get him to Grand Mound."

"I just hope Mike likes cherry pie," said Emmett, paying no attention. "One thing we do in Grand Mound is eat well, and, let me tell you, nobody bakes a better cherry pie than Tracy Ellen, unless of course it's her mother."

"Think you'll be able to stand all this?" asked Tracy Ellen, echoing my thoughts.

"Just telling the truth, the whole truth, and nothing but the truth," said Emmett. "Tracy Ellen can't deny she's won the Grand Mound High School Bake-off with her killer cherry pie, every year she's been in high school—even when she was a freshman. She bakes pie like a professional pastry chef."

"It will be a change for me to live in a home where there are women," I said, trying to be diplomatic. "My mom died when I was four, and my dad, younger brother, and I have been batching it ever since."

"That's what we heard," said Emmett, and I wondered briefly where he had heard it. But then I supposed whoever had scouted me must have checked into my family background too.

"What can you tell me about this job I have in the mornings?" I asked. "Do you know who I'll be working for?"

"Oh, didn't I say? You'll be working for me. I'm the independent insurance agent in Grand Mound. Got me a little office on Main Street, but somehow I end up doing most of my business from the house. Folks just drop by when the spirit moves them. As for your job, I don't expect you'll be asked to do anything a fellow who earned a BA in business management—with distinction, no less—can't handle," and he grinned again, letting me know that he knew almost everything there was to know about me.

I felt I should give him a quiz, like when a psychologist spits out words and the patient does free association.

"Byron," I'd say.

And he'd reply, "Your younger brother, a senior in computer science at De Paul University, named for the poet, because your brother was born with a deformed foot that had to be in a cast for the first year of his life."

"Sugar," I'd say.

And he'd reply, "Sherrylynne Espinoza, your first girlfriend."

And we'd go on like that, playing *This Is Your Life*, Mike Houle, until I found something that he didn't know about me.

I thought of a girl I was seriously involved with while I was at LSU. Her name was Francie Deveau, she was Cajun, slim, and dark-skinned with black eyes that seemed to be all pupil.

"Tell me something you've never told anyone else, something no one else in the world knows about you," Francie said to me one evening in my tiny room in what had once been a mansion, was now student housing, not far from the LSU campus. We were cuddled up in my single bed, having dragged the covers up off the floor after making love.

"Hurricane Francie," I said. "I think of you as Hurricane Francie, because you're such an uninhibited lover. But I've never had the nerve to say the words out loud."

"Oh, that's nice," Francie said, running the tip of her tongue along my upper lip like she was applying lipstick to it. "But I want something really secret, something dark and revealing. You must have a skeleton in your closet. Everyone does."

"Okay," I said. "Something I know about myself that I've never spoken aloud, tried never to think about. Something that no one else seems able to recognize. During a game, when I get into a tight situation, a crucial situation, I choke."

"That's not much of a skeleton," Francie said.

"For a baseball player it is."

In high school, the first girl who actually liked me back was Sugar Espinoza, one of a dozen or so students bussed to our mainly white, middle-class high school from a Puerto Rican neighborhood close to downtown Chicago.

She had beautiful long black hair and chocolate eyes. Her teeth were a sparkling white, and she wore a different lipstick every day, each brilliant as a tropical flower. Sugar wore tight sweaters and tighter jeans, and talked a mile a minute in a charming accent. She taught me about serious french kissing, and before long, about most other aspects of sex.

When I asked her for a date, Sugar said I couldn't come to her house to pick her up. Pick her up was a euphemism anyway, because I traveled by bus. After Mom was killed, Dad sold the car. We were within walking distance of work, school, and the downtown shops, what did we need a car for? It is only since both Byron and I have left home that Dad has started to drive again.

I'd take the bus into Chicago, meet Sugar on a street corner, and we'd take in a movie, usually a double feature at a second-run movie house, where we'd sit in the back row and kiss and put our hands down each other's jeans. And where, during a break, Sugar would light up a cigarette, and stare around the mostly empty theater as if daring anyone to complain.

After the movie we'd go for coffee or ice cream, then Sugar would head off on her own.

"I don' ever wan' to be seen in my neighborhood wit' joo. My old man, he'd have a monkey he ever seen me wit' an Anglo. He don' think I should go out wit' boys 'til I'm eighteen, then only wit' ones he pick out for me."

"He doesn't know you date?"

"He thinks I still play wit' dolls."

"Anatomically correct ones?"

"One of these nights, soon as my girlfriend's parents go out of town, we'll see how good joo play."

The next Friday night Sugar took my hand and said, "Come on! Violet's folks have gone to Detroit for the long weekend."

She led me about ten blocks in a direction we'd never gone, the neighborhood getting seedier each block.

"We'll cut down the alley," she said, pulling me along. "I know too many people might be out on the street."

We came in through a back yard crammed with junk, up a rickety iron fire escape at the back of a very old brick building. We entered by a fire door and walked down a long, dark hallway that creaked ominously at every step. The interior was like an old hotel, and it smelled like a basement with underlying odors of cabbage, urine, and perfume.

Sugar knocked on a black door and after she identified herself, the opener released about six chains and locks.

Violet was a lumpy-looking girl with frizzy hair and very thick glasses. The apartment was cozy, filled with furniture covered in colorful knitted shawls, and dime-store religious pictures, on the walls.

"Violet, this is Mike. We'll talk later."

I managed a quick wave at Violet before Sugar pulled me past the small television that Violet and two young children were watching, and straight into a bedroom.

We kissed wildly, then lay on the bed and undressed each other. There wasn't a lot to undress. Sugar was wearing a white sweater, jeans, and panties. When the sweater was off she pushed my head down to her breasts. I took each firm, orange-sized breast in my mouth, the nipple becoming rigid at the touch of my tongue. Sugar moaned appreciatively.

She pushed my head down farther. I undid her jeans and she helped me peel them and her panties off. She guided my mouth to the wetness between her legs.

"A little higher," Sugar moaned. "Oh, yeah," she said, as my tongue found what was like another tiny nipple. "Oh, yeah. Pretend your tongue's a butterfly. Let it flutter!"

She convulsed against my mouth, then shuddered wildly, and held my head in place with both hands.

"Don't stop," she whispered. "Turn around and I'll kiss you ' 'til you feel good, too."

And she did.

When she could feel me getting really excited, she pushed me away. "Now, make love wit' me."

I pulled myself around until I was above her. Her mouth was already on mine, the sweet tastes intermingling. But instead of entering her, as she was offering, I held back, because an alarm was beeping in my head—my father's warning about always being responsible . . . "If you're not responsible one way you'll sure as hell be responsible the other."

There was one family freedom Byron and I enjoyed that most sons didn't. We were always allowed to bring girlfriends to the house, night or day. Dad seldom had a girlfriend, and I can't recall one ever staying overnight.

"You've got to learn how to relate to women," Dad would say. Then he'd give us The Speech.

"If a woman thinks enough of you to make love with you, treat her kindly. Don't ever brag to your friends, no matter how much you want to, and always think good thoughts about her ever after.

"She's your responsibility." The Speech would go on. "It's your responsibility not to get her pregnant. You know how girls get pregnant, I've told you often enough. Intelligent girls will know about birth control. But you'll never go wrong if you assume every girl you're with knows nothing about birth control. That's your job, and don't you ever forget it."

I first heard The Speech when I was about eleven. Dad banged a box of condoms down on the kitchen table and demonstrated on a banana. If he was embarrassed he didn't show it, but I was mortified. I barely understood what part of my anatomy I was supposed to cover with the condom, and I certainly hadn't had any close encounters with girls, unless you could count Sally Pearlman putting her tongue in my mouth during a game of spin-the-bottle at her birthday party.

"Remember what I've said," Dad growled, rolling up the condom and fitting it back into the box. "We'll have this talk again in six months, just to refresh your memory."

As the years passed The Speech expanded to contain other information about sex. Because of The Speech, Byron and I became the neighborhood experts on sex. We were able to dispel most of the weird rumors started by boys who knew nothing but what they'd heard second-, third-, and fourth-hand from other boys.

With Sugar pulling me down on top of her, I frantically

reached one arm over the side of the bed, searching for my jeans and, the condom carefully concealed in the secret compartment of my wallet.

"What joo doing?"

"We need protection."

"A safe?"

"Yeah."

"What joo think, I'm stupid? There's a free clinic. I been on the pill since I was fourteen."

Later, after Sugar had guided me out of the neighborhood, while she was waiting with me for my bus, I made the mistake of asking what she had liked best about our evening together.

"The thrill of doing it and not getting caught," Sugar said. "My brothers'd kill joo if they found out. My old man would probably kill us both, if he thought I was fucking an Anglo."

Determined to stay alive, I brought Sugar to my home a couple of times after school. But the sex, while good, was never quite so good, perhaps because instead of lying and saying my father would gun us down without mercy if he caught us naked in my room, I told the truth and said that as long as I acted responsibly my father preferred that I brought my girlfriends home.

Sugar didn't find my bedroom thrilling enough, and I was too chicken to visit her neighborhood again, so we drifted apart. She dropped out our senior year to marry a guy named Kiko, a short, swarthy boy with a drooping mustache and a penchant for purple shirts and pointed black shoes.

Looking back, I haven't been very successful when it comes to flashy women. While I was at LSU I liked Louisiana girls with their mysterious bayou upbringings, their language full of words I found strange to the ear and tongue. For some reason I was attracted to women who enjoyed making love in dangerous situations, but thinking each sexual experience might be my last is not a turn-on for me. Once, about three in the morning, my date and I were walking across the foggy LSU campus when she leaned against a light standard in the shadow of the library, slipped off her shoes, stepped out of her panties and stuffed them in her purse, leaned against the pole, and said, "Make love to me."

"Are you kidding?" I asked, though I knew she wasn't.

"It's more fun when there's danger involved," she replied.

"Not for me," I said, and walked on.

"Chicken," said the girl, whose name I've blocked from my memory, with good reason.

Francie Deveau was my sweetheart for well over a year. We thought we were in love. We met in the library at LSU where she was obviously having a difficult time with elementary statistics. I volunteered my services as tutor.

Francie had blue-black hair to her waist, and a Cajun temper like a rolling thunderstorm. She was the first of her family—there were six brothers and sisters—to finish high school, let alone enter university. They lived in bayou country in a rambling, ramshackle house that would have been a perfect setting for a horror movie. The family didn't seem to work, or farm, or fish; they just existed on land that may or may not have been theirs. Her family, especially her three brothers, spoke with such heavy accents, I had to continually ask them to repeat themselves.

Her father had only one eye, and seemed to rule as part dictator, part priest, part social worker. Before breakfast my first morning there on a visit, he offered a free-fall prayer that was more of sermon, the kind delivered on television by evangelical zealots. He called on God to smite his enemies and to protect his family from, and I quote, "the terrors of the outside world," a phrase spoken while looking directly at me with his one red eye. He called down plagues and pestilence on his enemies, of whom it appeared there were many. I was an object of curiosity, like an unexotic animal that had suddenly appeared on their doorstep, led on a string by their daughter.

Francie and I had arrived late the previous night, after a bus ride to the end of the line, where we were met by one of her brothers, then a wild trip in a pickup truck, and finally a motorboat cruise through a midnight-black swamp.

The prayer raged on, one of Francie's sisters chiming in an "Amen" whenever her father stopped to take a breath. I thought of the previous night. I was put in a bedroom on the second floor, and after I'd been asleep for some time, I was wakened by Francie crawling under the covers with me. As I listened to the prayer I imagined my bound body being pushed over the side of a pirogue into a scummy bayou by Francie's brothers while her father wildly denounced fornicators to the heavens.

I lived in fear the rest of that eternally long weekend, even after I insisted that Francie stay in her own room the next night.

When we got back to LSU, Francie said she thought we ought to stop seeing each other. She and her family had decided that I just wouldn't fit in. I was too different.

I hastily agreed before she changed her mind.

EIGHT

The Buick glided over the two-lane, through the rolling Iowa countryside. Emmett had been talking while my mind was wandering. When I tuned him in again he was saying: "There's a freight stops in Grand Mound about 10:30 at night, farmers think nothing of dropping by the house at 11:30 to insure a tractor or cultivator that arrived on the late freight. Sometimes two or three separate items come in on the train. The street in front of our house looks like a scene from a horror movie where the locals, at night with torches, hunt down the monster.

"Grand Mound certainly isn't the fast lane, but we live well, Mike. I'm planning to retire at sixty-two, just ten years from now. The agency will be a fine business for a young enterprising . . ."

"Emmett! The boy hasn't even seen Grand Mound yet. Don't be trying to sell him your insurance business," Marge Powell said from the back seat. When I turned toward her, she said to me, "You'll have to forgive him, Mike. Emmett and his friends— you'll hear about the Grand Mound Booster Club soon enough— are so enthusiastic about small-town life that sometimes it's a little frightening."

"Did you know, Mike," Emmett picked right up, "Iowa has more small towns for its size and population than any other state? Some people claim there was once a town about every mile, on every secondary highway in the state, but now the farms are getting larger and the farmers are getting fewer. When the farmers go, the small towns die. We're trying, me and my friends, to reverse that trend.

"We don't have to worry about Grand Mound dying for a

few years," Emmett went on, and the way he smiled I knew that was his way of using understatement.

"Grand Mound is one of the few towns in Iowa to show an increase in population every year for the past five years. Now the increase isn't all that much, but when you consider Iowa had the largest decline in population of any state during that time, the fact that our population now is about the same as it was fifteen or twenty years ago speaks well for our energy and ingenuity."

He smiled again, as if he was delivering a lecture to a Chamber of Commerce luncheon. "We're recovering, while almost every other town I know of is still losing population. And I believe one of the prime reasons we're prospering is having a team in the Cornbelt League. You'd be surprised at how many of our players decide to become full-time residents in Grand Mound."

"No, I don't think I would," I said.

"What happens in small towns, or at least towns where the elders, as me and my friends like to think of ourselves, look out for the future of the inhabitants, the situation becomes positively tribal . . ."

"Oh, Emmett, don't go delivering your lecture. Mike just isn't ready for that sort of thing," said Marge.

"Tribal," Emmett went on. "The people of the town become a loose co-operative, jointly looking after their best interests, just as primitive tribes rallied together to fend off enemies."

"Daddy, you talk as though we're being besieged."

"Only an analogy, my dear. What I mean is that a fine, well-managed small town displays tribal tendencies, not the least of which is the need to bring new blood into the community, which is what we accomplish by having a team in the Cornbelt League and bringing upstanding young men like Mike into our community, a certain percentage of whom will remain in Grand Mound, assimilate into the community, marry . . ."

"I believe I get the picture," I said.

"Not the whole picture, Mike. We'll show you that slowly, a bit at a time."

"I'm sure you will," I said.

We stopped for coffee and pie. We'd no sooner sat ourselves in booth when Emmett asked the waitress, "Do you know the perfect name for a waitress?" The girl looked blankly at him. "Phyllis," he said, and laughed loudly. And, when the girl continued to stare at him like he was an escaped mental patient, "Phyllis. Fill Us!"

The girl made a face. Tracy Ellen and Marge groaned.

"I've got a million of 'em," said Emmett, slapping my shoulder.

"More than that," said Tracy Ellen, looking for meaning in the ice in her water glass.

The land around Grand Mound is rolling and hilly. I didn't ask, for fear of getting a two-hour history lecture from Emmett, but I suppose the largest hill, the one where the Powells' home sits, is the grand mound the town is named for.

The Powells live on a tree-lined street in a two-story, white, frame home with a big front porch, complete with porch swing and white-enameled table and chairs. My room is on the second floor, large and bright with double windows facing east, a walk in closet as big as my room at university, a huge double bed, and polished hardwood floors.

My first evening in Grand Mound.

No sooner had I cleaned up and unpacked my few clothes and possessions than I was called to dinner. I've been to restaurant buffets where there was less food on the table. There was roast pork and roasted potatoes, thick, pan-browned gravy, creamed cauliflower, fresh peas the color of outfield grass, and some orange mush that Mrs. Powell said was yams.

I passed on the yams, but I ate a couple of helpings of everything else, which included salad, three kinds of pickles, a relish or two, fresh dinner rolls, and applesauce for the pork. I washed it down with several glasses of iced tea. Then, in spite of my protests, Emmett forced a partial third helping on me. After which there was cherry pie and ice cream, and I was offered a choice of tea, coffee, cocoa, or something else I'd never heard of, called Ovaltine.

"What teams are in the Cornbelt League?" I asked Emmett, while I was accepting a second piece of pie and ice cream from Tracy Ellen. We had adjourned to the living room. "I'm afraid my agent didn't tell me much."

"Not likely you've ever heard of the teams, unless, of course, you're a scholar of small-town Iowa. Just a row of little towns, dots on the map, scattered along Highway 30. There's Mount Vernon, Lisbon, Mechanicsville, Wheatland, Clarence, DeWitt, and of course, Grand Mound."

"That's seven teams," I said. "Makes it difficult for the schedule-maker."

"Makes for three games every night of the summer," said Emmett jovially. DeWitt is the biggest town, right around five thousand people, Mount Vernon's next with about four thousand, us and Wheatland have roughly fifteen hundred residents. Of course, each town also has a rural population base to draw from.

"The bigger towns use some local talent. At first we had to import almost our whole team, but this year you're one of only five new players. Grand Mound has a lot to offer, Mike. Most of the fellows who come back for a second season settle down in Grand Mound—in fact, several players just stayed right on when their first season ended. They'd made so many friends and attachments there was never a reason to leave. Several of them have married local girls."

As Emmett beamed at me, his eyes moved to Tracy Ellen, sitting beside him on the sofa, balancing her plate on her knee. She was wearing pastel-pink shorts and top, her tiny feet encased in white sneakers with pink inlays and pink laces. There was something about those tiny, pink-clad feet that touched my heart.

"How long has the Cornbelt League operated? I've honestly never heard of it. I took a quick glance at the *Sporting News*, but didn't see it mentioned. And how long has Grand Mound had a team?"

"Oh, the league's been around for fifty years at least. We're unaffiliated, outside of organized baseball, which is why the *Sporting News* doesn't write us up. But we play great baseball, Mike. And Grand Mound has had a team for, oh, several years."

I asked him to name me a player or two who had gone on to the Bigs or even to Triple A, but he just smiled broadly again and said, "You'll like the other players, Mike. Most of them are college boys like yourself."

It was interesting to spend an evening with the Powells. There was a TV set in the living room but it never got turned on. We just talked. Or Emmett, and sometimes Marge talked, while Tracy Ellen and I listened and made occasional comments.

There was a late evening snack for all of us, more cherry pie

77

and ice cream, served up with more praise from Emmett for Tracy Ellen's baking, which I have to admit is the best I've ever tasted. It's as if they knew cherry pie was my favorite food in the world. And all the Powells mentioned a couple of times each that I was free to raid the refrigerator any time I wanted to.

Afterwards, Emmett and I stepped out onto the front porch. The humidity was a shock, all evening an unobtrusive air conditioner had kept us comfortable. We stood and stared off into the thick, firefly-peppered darkness. I heard the porch swing creak as Emmett eased down onto it.

We remained quiet for some time. Somewhere far away a dog yelped. The heat seemed touchable, velvety, and the smell of honeysuckle so powerful I could taste it.

"I want to show you something," Emmett said. He rose from the porch swing and picked his way down the three concrete steps to the driveway. He beckoned for me to follow in that instant before he became just another shadow amidst the moon-gilded leaves of the tall honeysuckle bushes.

I felt my way to the passenger side of the car and got in. Emmett drove the few blocks to Highway 30, not turning on the lights until we were at least a block from the house. The highway was a ribbon of blackness winding between equally black fields, planting having finished for the season.

"What I'm gonna show you," said Emmett, "are small-town baseball fields. The other teams do their practicing at night, some play inter-squad games, some play the occasional pre-season game against the other league teams, especially on the weekends. This being a Monday is Grand Mound's night off. You'll be playing in an inter-squad game tomorrow night.

"If you hadn't had to get up early to catch your flight, and if this wasn't your first night here, why we could have scouted the opposition. Every second town we pass will have a ballpark lit up like Times Square. From a distance some of them look like fire on the ocean. . . . I tell you, Mike, there is nothing like the lights of a ballpark against a star-filled night sky," and his voice trailed off. He obviously wanted to say more, words failing him.

He was right. There were no words to convey what we saw. Suddenly, we would take a sweeping turn into a town, and there on one side or other of the highway, like a burst of fireworks, would be the ballpark. Or, as we rolled along, a park would bloom like a giant marigold out of the sensitive blue-black night. We would catch a glimpse of the emerald grass, perhaps a flash of white uniform, before we would be gone again, the lights of the ballpark behind us, as if we were driving into ink.

The next town would be subdued, a twinkle of streetlight the only illumination, and Emmett would point out the empty ballpark, huddled like a huge, sleeping animal curled against the night. Then we would press on, watching the horizon for the golden aura of another ballpark, another flood of sunflower light.

"Small towns," Emmett sighed, as he pulled off the highway, to turn toward home.

NINE

My first full day in Grand Mound.

In the morning, after a breakfast offering more variety than most cafés, we got ready to head for the office. I had not had many occasions to wear a suit, though I had acquired a dark blue one and a pair of black shoes for my graduation from LSU.

"I feel like an organ grinder's monkey," I said. "Do I look too out of place?"

"Oh, you look just fine, Mike," Marge Powell said. "Very handsome."

I didn't believe her. "Sure, this suit and tie won't stand out like a sore thumb here in Grand Mound."

"You can buy a casual jacket or a light suit with your first pay check," Emmett said, "but I think that Wall Street suit might be just what we're looking for," and he smiled across the breakfast table. "We like to find a suitable nickname for every player. How does Wall Street Mike Houle sound? I'll mention that to Dilly Eastwick, I bet he'd go for it."

"Dilly Eastwick is the newspaper editor," Tracy Ellen said. "You'll meet him soon enough. He's everywhere, pops up like a bad penny. Sometimes Daddy swears Dilly Eastwick can be in two or three places at once."

Emmett was reading the morning paper, an eight-page effort he'd retrieved from the front porch.

"Grand Mound is one of the smallest towns in America to have a daily newspaper. The *Grand Mound Leader* publishes six days a week. Dilly Eastwick came up here from Atlanta when I was just a boy. He bought the printing shop and the weekly newspaper. He convinced the town council to budget a subscription to the *Leader* into the property taxes. Those paid subscriptions enabled Dilly to create several jobs at the newspaper, and, over the years, almost every boy in Grand Mound, and nowadays girls too, deliver papers for the *Leader*. "Tracy Ellen delivered for a few months. Dilly sees that the routes are never more than fifty papers, so a good number of young people get to earn some spending money."

"Look there," said Tracy Ellen, peering over her father's shoulder, "there's your photograph, Mike."

I walked around and stood beside her. And there I was, my graduation photo from LSU, cap and gown and all. The story was headlined: NEW BASEBALL PLAYERS ARRIVE, and beneath were photographs of myself and a dark-haired boy in a baseball cap, named Daniel Morgenstern, who hailed from New Jersey. The third player was from San Francisco, Stanley Wood. Apparently there was no photograph of Stanley Wood available.

"Those other fellows arrived a couple of days ago," Emmett said. "It says here," Emmett went on, now reading aloud, "that you like cherry pie, the Chicago Cubs, and pretty blonde girls whose initials are Tracy Ellen Powell. . . ."

"Emmett, for goodness' sakes!" said Marge. "You will embarrass this boy to death, not to mention Tracy Ellen."

I peered closely at the short paragraph about each player. The part about the Cubs and cherry pie *was* there.

As we left for work, Marge and Tracy Ellen stood on the front porch and waved to us as Emmett backed the car out of the driveway. It was a nice thing to do, I thought. Tracy Ellen was wearing jeans and a sunflower-yellow jacket with GMHS in black capitals across the front.

Powell Real Estate and Insurance occupied half of a small, white-painted building with green shutters on Main Street. The other half housed a barber shop. The building had a false front like something out of a western movie set. The office consisted of three very old wooden desks, each one buried under a mound of papers, three filing cabinets, and a table holding a coffee maker. The floors were yellow hardwood, and the office smelled of floor wax and accumulated paper. The front window was tinted blue to keep out the morning sun.

"You're a business major, Mike, so you'll know the answer to this question. What economic factor most affects the cost of balloons?" A pause. "Inflation. Ha!"

We did little work that morning. In fact, we didn't do any work. Emmett assigned me the smallest desk, explaining that he had a secretary who came in three half-days a week to do clerical work and bookkeeping.

Fifteen minutes after we arrived, there were five visitors in the office, none of them there to buy insurance or real estate. I'd watched them cautiously crossing the street toward us, as if they were coming on the scene of an accident, their collective purpose apparently to get a look at and appraise the new second-base man.

More people arrived. There were several conversations going on simultaneously. I smiled and tried to remember to shake hands firmly. I tried to look like a second-base man. I was even asked to sign a couple of autographs, one for a very old woman who had a thick velvet-covered autograph book in which she claimed to have the autograph of every player who ever appeared in a Grand Mound uniform.

Emmett had a new joke.

He told it to everyone as they entered the office. "How do you define dual air bags? A political debate."

From one snippet of the conversation I overheard, a family named Lindfors was very unhappy with the ballplayer assigned to them. Was it Daniel Morgenstern they were unhappy with? There was no question, just from the photograph in the newspaper, that Daniel Morgenstern was Jewish. Would that be a problem here in Grand Mound? Surely not, though the minority population of the area would be almost nonexistent.

But the word that reoccurred in the conversation sounded to me like "Chinese." Who would be Chinese? Certainly not Daniel Morgenstern, nor anyone named Stanley Wood, nor me. Maybe one of the previous newcomers was Chinese.

After another fifteen minutes, when the office got positively crowded, Emmett placed a small, well-worn sign inside the glass of the door: BACK IN 5 MINUTES. Why did I have the feeling that sign hung on the door for hours at a time?

With Emmett leading the way we moved *en masse* across the street to the Doll House Café where, I suspected, the other half of the population of Grand Mound and vicinity was congregated. I must have met over a hundred people before we headed home for lunch.

There was a constantly fluctuating crowd in the café. A farmer in bib overalls, a townsman in shirtsleeves, or a middle-aged woman obviously dressed in church-going finery, would sit at our table welcoming me to Grand Mound, but eyeing me ever so carefully, as if trying to discern my ability to play second base by the way I sipped coffee, or the angle at which I held my fork when eating cherry pie.

For, yes, I hadn't even pulled my chair up to the table when a waitress appeared with a piece of cherry pie à la mode.

"Mrs. Nesbitt heard this is your favorite," said the waitress, who was dark and pretty, with a twitchy smile that showed off twin dimples like stars on either side of her mouth. She sat the pie and a glass of milk in front of me. I'd later find out from Emmett that her name was Nan Hurchubise. I exchanged the milk for coffee.

The visitors at our table changed about every two minutes.

Emmett would introduce them, they'd eye me, ask me a couple of questions, mainly, "How do you like Grand Mound?" They would then move on to another table, or out of the café altogether. Names went in one ear and out the other. I smiled and shook hands. It both pleased and puzzled me that the mere arrival of a new second-base man could generate so much enthusiasm.

The café owner, Mrs. Nesbitt, a large, jolly woman in her fifties, came and sat with us. She offered me early lunch, or more cherry pie. When I declined she forced seconds on me anyway

"How did you know about me liking cherry pie?" I asked her. "I've been in town less than a day."

"Well, you show me a twenty-three-year-old boy from the Midwest who *doesn't* like cherry pie, that will be the oddity."

There was a flurry of activity at the door as a tall, hawk-faced man entered, accompanied by Daniel Morgenstern. They sat at a table across from us and the emphasis shifted to them.

"Come on over and I'll introduce you," said Emmett. "That's Dr. Greenspan and the new catcher, Daniel Morgenstern. The Greenspans will be Daniel's family while he's playing in Grand Mound."

"Don't tell me," I said. "The Greenspans have an eligible daughter."

Emmett cleared his throat.

"Well, they do have a daughter; but she's only a junior in high school. There was some discussion about whether they should take Daniel in, Becky being so young. That is . . . well, it's really just a coincidence that they have a daughter."

As soon as he entered the café I knew I'd seen Dr. Greenspan before—at the Cedar Rapids Airport. I suspect I'd also seen Mrs.

Greenspan, and that Becky was the beautiful, dusky-skinned girl with them. Were they there to get a preview of me? Why had Emmett lied about knowing them when I'd asked about the people I thought were staring at me?

"I hope you young men will be friends," Dr. Greenspan said, shaking my hand.

"Be nice to Dr. G," Emmett said, "he's the only doctor for miles. He treats all your aches and pains and muscle pulls. In fact he treats the whole team and never sends a bill."

"A small contribution," said Dr. Greenspan.

I told Daniel I'd see him at practice. It was going to be a pleasure to talk alone with some of the other players and find out if something weird was going on, or if this town was just populated by overly enthusiastic sports nuts.

I had to admit the latter was possible, as every person I spoke to assured me they'd be at the practice scheduled for 2:00 P.M. What kind of town comes out in the afternoon to watch their baseball team practice?

"It's a shame," one of the farmers, in railroad overalls and a red Orkin cap, said as he was describing the ballpark, "for all that outfield grass to go to waste. I've been lobbying for twenty years to have my cows graze the outfield one day a week, all summer, no charge. My cows would do a better job than that expensive tractor-mower, and they could get rid of that useless groundskeeper."

He was hooted down. I suspect the observation was being made for my benefit, for he laughed heartily at his own joke.

I smiled politely.

It turned out the joke was also directed at the groundskeeper, a tall, heavyset man with coppery hair, wearing overalls faded to the pale shade of a noontime sky, and sitting at a corner table.

"You reckon you could train your cows to leave the infield grass along the third-base line about a half-inch longer than the rest so when our team bunts up there the ball has a better chance of staying fair?" asked the groundskeeper and laughed heartily.

I recognized the groundskeeper. I wondered if he recognized me, then wondered if I wanted him to.

TEN

Lunch with my family. Tracy Ellen came home from the high school, Emmett and I from downtown. Marge had prepared pork chops, three vegetables, two salads, raisin pie, and ice cream.

"I hope you don't mind if I take it easy on the food," I said to Marge. "It's not a reflection on your cooking, but I've been eating since daybreak, and if I eat another big meal I won't be able to move on the field."

"This is a light meal, Mike," Emmett said, grinning jovially. "Only one pork chop each, hardly enough to ward off starvation, but I understand your situation. We'll feed you a big meal after the game."

Emmett drove me to the ballpark. A white-on-green sign out front said "Fred Noonan Field."

"Who was Fred Noonan?" I asked Emmett, as we were walking across the parking lot. "Someone who built the stadium? A local hero?"

"Neither of the above," said Emmett. "Guess you didn't study history at university."

"I didn't," I said. "Was he a vice president?"

"No, sir. Fred Noonan is the answer to one of the best trivia questions of all time. You ever hear of Amelia Earhart?"

"She was a lady pilot. Kind of like Lindbergh. She disappeared on a round-the-world flight back in the thirties."

"Ah," said Emmett, smiling, proud to be educating me. "But Amelia Earhart wasn't alone when she disappeared. So who was Amelia Earhart's navigator? Who disappeared with her out around Howland Island in the South Pacific?"

"Fred Noonan?" I ventured.

"I knew you weren't born yesterday, Mike."

"But why him? Was he from this part of Iowa?"

Emmett seemed surprised by that question. "Oh, I don't think so," he said. I think he was from out west somewhere, maybe California, though Amelia was from Kansas, not that far from here. No, when we came to name the new stadium there were lots of suggestions, like Bob Feller Park and John Wayne Park; they're both famous Iowans you know.

"This naming was done, oh, maybe twenty years ago. Before that it was simply known as the ballpark. I guess it was Dilly Eastwick decided the ballpark needed a real name. It was Dilly started the Grand Mound Booster Club. It was Dilly brought up the name change at a booster club meeting.

"In his position as editor of the *Grand Mound Leader,* Dilly held a contest. People suggested other Iowa athletes, politicians, educators—Herbert Hoover was right up there. And they suggested generic names like Veterans' Stadium and Memorial Stadium.

"The arguments at the Doll House were starting to get downright mean-spirited. Folks claimed to have been in safer barroom brawls. Some people got so touchy it looked like there'd be permanent enemies made. There was a small but vociferous faction wanted to name the park Johnny Carson Stadium, because he was so popular at the time, though he was born in Nebraska. It was Dilly Eastwick suggested Fred Noonan Field, as a sort of compromise.

"'He's one of America's forgotten men.' Dilly said. 'Why, all the world knows Amelia Earhart, but you won't find one in a thousand can name the man disappeared off the face of the earth with her. I bet there isn't anything else in the world named for Fred Noonan. No, sir, our baseball stadium will be unique.'

"And because there were so many choices and people were so divided, Fred Noonan won on the third ballot. I don't think anyone's ever been sorry. The name is a great conversation starter, and all the children in Grand Mound learn about Amelia Earhart and Fred Noonan in fourth grade. We're the only school in America teaches a whole week on those two people."

The Grand Mound baseball stadium sat about a block back from the secondary highway. Stadium is perhaps too grand a word, though the field was picture perfect, obviously lovingly tended. The park itself was small as a button, the fences at the foul lines 298 feet, though at its farthest point the center-field wall was almost four hundred feet from home plate.

We entered through the front gate, just like paying customers, and made our way under the stands. There is little that hasn't been said about the thrill of walking into a beautiful ballpark. And Fred Noonan Field was beautiful. The grass had been recently cut and was perfectly groomed. The air was filled with the aromas of fresh-cut grass and sunshine to such an extent that I found myself inhaling deeply as I made my way toward the first-base dugout. The dressing rooms were standard-issue concrete block, with chipped apple-green benches along each wall. The lockers were metal, standard high-school olive-drab. The locker room gave up the usual odors of sweat, disinfectant, and urine. Emmett gave me a new bicycle lock to place on my locker.

"We supply the first lock," said Emmett. "If you lose it you have to buy the replacement."

The Grand Mound team was called the Greenshirts. The home-team uniforms were a stark enamel-white with kelly-green trim, numbers, and names; our road uniforms were kelly green with white trim. Every time I've suited up ever since Little League, it's always a thrill to pick up my uniform top and see my name, HOULE, in bright letters across the back.

Just as well; baseball players are amused by small things, and one of the favorite tricks in high school and college is to hang another player's jersey in someone's locker. If he doesn't check it before he puts it on, he's in big trouble. I've even seen this happen at the major-league level. I once saw outfielder Ivan Calderon of the White Sox play about three innings wearing a relief pitcher's name and number on his back.

One year at LSU, we had a bat girl for our home games. Three of us arranged with the equipment manager to take the uniform of a large, redneck outfielder who continually gave the young bat girl, our hitting coach's daughter, a bad time. Instead of his name and number, we had BAT GIRL and double zeroes sewn on the back. I kept him distracted as he was dressing. For whatever reason, the fans—we were hosting Mississippi State— cooperated. He played the top of the first in the outfield. When he came to bat, the umpire pointed out he wasn't wearing the number that had been announced over the public-address system and tossed him.

* * * * *

In the Grand Mound locker room I was introduced to many players. Most of the names went by like straws in the wind. If I'd been given a test I'd have been able to supply names or positions for only a couple of the players, one of whom certainly did look Chinese. Unfortunately someone yelled as he was introduced, and I didn't catch his name.

I met the other two new players, an outfielder named Barry McMartin, and a pitcher named Crease Fowler.

"I bet the family you've been assigned to just happens to have an eligible daughter," I said to Fowler.

"Yeah. And they're anxious for us to date. Usually parents aren't thrilled about their daughters hanging out with itinerant baseball players."

"You, too?" I asked Barry McMartin.

"I should be so lucky," he replied. 'My 'family' only has sons, and they're away at college. I had to look through a six-foot stack of photo albums last night. Man, there's something weird about this town."

I paid particular attention to a player named Bobby Manuela, the shortstop I'd be working with. He was Mexican, about twenty-five, small, with a ready smile and quick brown eyes.

"This is my third year in Grand Mound," he said. "I live here all the time now. Brought my wife and baby here after the first season. My second daughter was born here."

"Bobby works at the Co-op," said Emmett, who was sticking to me like a shadow. "He manages the hardware department."

Then I was introduced to the Greenshirts manager, Gene Walston, and his assistant, Vince Singletary.

"We play a lot of inter-squad games getting ready for the season," Emmett said. "Gene and Vince take turns managing the opposing teams."

"Step into my office a minute, Mike. I want to have a quick word with you," Gene Walston said. He was a gaunt-cheeked man in his late fifties, his shoulders a little stooped. His assistant, Vince Singletary, must have weighed close to three hundred pounds, which he carried well on a six-foot-six frame, except for a more than comfortable swelling in the area of his belt. Singletary was black as a bowling ball. I knew I was going to like him even before he spoke. His smile was like sunshine, his laugh lines deep.

Emmett and I began to follow Walston out of the dressing room.

"Mike only," Walston said to Emmett. Emmett reluctantly stayed where he was.

The manager's office consisted of a battered desk and an even more battered filing cabinet that looked as if it had absorbed the rage of a thousand one-run losses.

"Just a little confidence strictly between you and me, Mike. Don't pass this on to anyone, especially Emmett. As far as I'm concerned you've got the starting second-base spot locked up. I had a friend videotape four games at LSU. You're a class act, young fellow. You field like a cat and hit like a bandit. Just wanted you to know that. So, relax, no pressure, Mike, the job's yours."

I barely had time to say thank you before we were walking back down the hall to the clubhouse.

There was no direct access to the dugouts on the first- and third-base sides. When we were dressed we entered the field from a single door behind home plate, and walked either right or left according to which uniform had been assigned us.

The stadium seated over two thousand, with small open bleachers on the first- and third-base sides, and a slightly larger area of covered seating behind home plate. The park was surrounded by a twelve-foot-high wooden fence, painted a dark green. All along the inside of the fence were bright ads, in reds, greens, and yellows, mainly advertising Grand Mound businesses. The largest sign, about forty feet long, stretching across left-center field, had red letters on a white background: EMMETT POWELL: YOUR INDEPENDENT INSURANCE AGENT IN GRAND MOUND.

I commented on the immaculate condition of the field. Emmett was still on the field, even though I was now warming up by playing catch with Bobby Manuela. A number of "family" members were on the field and sidelines, more or less accompanying their players.

"Yes, sir, we take pride in providing a little jewel of a playing field," said Emmett. "You can thank Roger, the groundskeeper, for that."

He beckoned the carrotty-haired groundskeeper over to us. "Runs the infield dirt through a flour sifter," Emmett said, when he introduced us.

"Proud to meet you, son," Roger Cash said, giving no indication that he had ever seen me before. I did likewise. "I'll do my best to make the infield around second base flat and true. You won't get any surprise bounces on any field I tend."

"Thank you," I said.

"Trouble is," Roger Cash went on, "what's sauce for the goose is sauce for the gander, as they say. If the ball bounces true for you it will do the same for your opponents."

A green Grand Mound baseball cap sat atop Cash's coppercolored hair, which spilled down over the collar of his white shirt. He glanced at me, then at Emmett, a wicked smile in his golden eyes.

"When you get to playing serious games, why, Emmett and I have come up with a plan to give you an edge, a tiny one. Not that you need one, Mike. But as they say, every little bit helps. Let's walk."

At the dugout, we three looked around conspiratorially, as Cash continued. "Now, if we were to look under the bench here—" As he spoke he bent over and peered under the double plank bench. "Well, look at what I found."

Running his fingers against the concrete wall behind the bench he came up with a half dozen pebbles, about the size of marbles.

"These are yours, Mike," he said, dumping the pebbles into my outstretched hand.

"As you leave the field after your opponent's first at-bat, you scatter them on the dirt. Next inning you do a little groundskeeping, pick them all up and keep them in a pocket until the inning is over, then you scatter them again. If you're lucky, your opponent will get one bad bounce a game."

"Sometimes that's all it takes to decide a game," said Emmett, slapping my shoulder.

"A ballplayer's like a race horse, needs every edge he can get," said Roger Cash.

"I don't know," I said.

"In baseball, whatever you don't get caught at is fair," said Roger Cash. "Players steal signs. Use the hidden-ball trick. Isn't written anywhere that a groundskeeper can't have a favorite player."

"I bet you say that to all the players."

"Mind you, you won't start until the season opens, no edges in inter-squad games," said Emmett.

"You know, I'm glad to see you have a little larceny in your hearts. I was beginning to think Grand Mound was too perfect," I said. "By the way, does this happen to have anything to do with distances?" Emmett looked puzzled.

Roger Cash smiled and a look passed between us. My guess was he was holding back because he wasn't certain I'd wanted to acknowledge our past relationship. He was about to speak when Emmett broke in.

"I know I've certainly got a favorite player," said Emmett, again slapping me on the shoulder. "You are gonna be a star in the Cornbelt League, my friend, and it will be a pleasure for me to contribute in some small way to your success."

"I'll go along if you guys say so," I said. "How big a discount does Mr. Cash get on his insurance?" I asked, joking, but seeing the expressions on both their faces I realized I'd stumbled on the truth. I carefully put the pebbles back under the bench.

Fred Noonan's Town

ELEVEN

As we began our warm-ups I was amazed to see the stands filling just as if a regular game was scheduled. Behind the covered grandstand the concessions were dispensing hot dogs, ice cream, and soda. There were more than a thousand people out to watch the afternoon practice.

We had a perfectly routine workout: calisthenics, wind sprints, stretching exercises, batting, fielding, and base-running practice. The squad was larger than I would have anticipated, over thirty players, with a preponderance of pitchers.

The manager's name, Gene Walston, had been bouncing around like a ping pong ball inside my head ever since we had been introduced. He was a slim, greying man with slightly stooped shoulders and a complexion like concrete. He didn't look at all familiar, but I knew that name.

About the time I took my position at second base to field some grounders, it came to me. *Suicide* Walston! He had been a third-base coach in the Bigs with a variety of clubs. His nickname grew out of his propensity to wave runners around third no matter how slim their chances of scoring.

He once got to manage the final fifty games of a season after the manager suffered a heart attack. But the team blew a five-game lead, lost the division, and Walston was gone from the Bigs, disappeared like a Mafia informer.

Walston's demise was helped along by a national pre-game baseball show that put together a collection of his blunders as third-base coach. I remember watching Walston at third frantically waving in runners who were doomed to be cut down by thirty feet. The camera showed him sending a runner home while in the background the shortstop was already taking the cutoff throw and firing toward the plate.

So this was what had become of Suicide Walston—which led me to speculate about Walston's decision to award me the starting second-base man's job. The other second-base man, John Quist, was a year or two older than me and a better fielder, though not as fast on the bases. But the way he whacked a couple of balls off the center-field scoreboard told me he certainly had more power than I did.

The practice broke up at about 4:00 P.M.

"Be back at 6:30 P.M.," said Walston. "The inter-squad game begins at 7:00 P.M. sharp."

As we drove home for supper, Emmett praised me as if I'd gotten the game-winning hit and made an unassisted triple play in the field. The reception at home was about the same. Tracy Ellen was sitting on the porch swing reading a book as we drove up, and Emmett began talking to her before he was fully out of the car.

"You should have seen Mike at second base this afternoon, Tracy Ellen. He was like an octopus out there. An octopus. Picked up every ball within a half block. And hit! At one point Mike hit five consecutive ground balls straight back up the middle. Keeps that up he'll bat .400."

"That's really nice," Tracy Ellen said, hardly raising her eyes from her book, a novel by someone named Tim Sandlin.

But as we were walking into the house—Emmett had his hand on the front doorknob and was hollering, "Marge, Marge, you'll never guess what Mike did at practice"—Tracy Ellen set the book down, stood up and said, "Congratulations, Mike. I'm glad you did well." Then she hugged me. I suppose it was the way a sister would hug a brother who had just played a good game of baseball, but frankly, her action surprised the hell out of me. Now, I don't know what to think about Tracy Ellen.

In the kitchen, Marge hugged me, too, and then we sat down to another meal fit for a threshing crew.

In spite of their protests I ate lightly.

"If I eat any more I'll run like I'm wearing cement blocks instead of cleats. I'll get caught stealing every time."

Emmett reluctantly agreed that he didn't want me to bog down.

"But I promise I'll go three rounds with that roast beef after the game," I told Marge.

"Good. I'll heat it up just as soon as the game's over," Marge said.

"Just a couple of sandwiches. I'm quite capable of making my own. I've fended for myself in the kitchen most of my life. You already cook three meals a day, Marge. I can't have you making a fourth on my account."

"Tracy Ellen and I will be just so pleased to make a meal for you after the game. This is the first time we've boarded a player, so we'll just have to get used to your hours."

The Powells seem like the happiest family I've ever met.

I guess I've always had some doubts about traditional families, because what I'd seen of family life, outside of our home where it was Dad's superhuman efforts that made our life good, it wasn't all it was cracked up to be.

Mom's sister, my Aunt Nadia, was married to an ignorant ox of a man named Ed Vlasyk. Ed worked at a foundry, flopped into a chair and turned on the TV the second he got home, and spent his evenings swilling beer and swatting at any child that got too close to him.

"So, Mike, you still hitting home runs or what?" was his standard greeting. I was surprised he remembered my name.

"I play second base. I don't hit many home runs," became my standard reply. Uncle Ed, sitting like a rock in his chair, would grunt and turn his attention back to his beer can.

"How come Aunt Nadia married a creep like him?" I asked Dad once. We were driving home after a Sunday afternoon visit. I liked to look at Aunt Nadia, she had the same flaming red hair as Mom, even though she was shorter, heavier, and seemed worn down by life.

"When you're young there's no way to guess how your life is gonna turn out. Ed and I went to school together. He wasn't a bad guy. We even used to double date once in a while. But life is full of cruel surprises, and Ed's way of coping is silence and beer. It's too bad."

"But why does he have a wife and kids if he doesn't like them?" I persisted. "If Aunt Nadia died he'd give the kids to the first person who'd have them. He'd never stick with them the way you've done."

I hugged Dad's arm.

"I can't explain, Mike. Maybe it's his fault. Maybe it was the way he was raised. Maybe he and Nadia just don't connect the way Gracie and I did. What is it they say? Don't judge a man until you've walked a mile in his shoes."

But I wasn't satisfied. In school, everyone, including the teachers, thought it odd that I came from a motherless home,

"So, how come you don't get married again?" I asked Dad

"Son, I've thought about it." Dad had kind of a crooked half-smile on his face. "I've even looked around a bit." He paused for a minute, ran a heavy hand over his dark chin. "You'd be surprised at how many women are interested in an ugly old guy like me. Lots of women who are divorced or separated, and anxious to have another go at the very thing that's made their lives miserable. And they're willing to settle for less than the best, just to have a man around the house. Now marriage to your Mom was the best thing that ever happened to me, and if I was to get married again it would have to be at least that good.

"The more I see of what's available the less interest I have in remarrying. Your Mom and I were together for eight years all told, we had something real special going and I wouldn't trade those eight years for all the women ever made.

"I never considered for a second letting somebody else raise you guys. And I think that has to do with your mom, too. Every time I look at you and Byron I see the half of you that's Gracie, and when you smile, or Byron laughs, or when either one of you stands with your hands on your hips when you're angry, the way Gracie used to do, why I see her all over again, and it's as if she isn't dead at all.

"Besides, if I was to bring another woman to live in this house, I'd probably have to take down your mom's photographs, and I can't stand the thought of that. If I ever find a woman I'd do that for, then I guess I'll know it's time."

TWELVE

The inter-squad game was so much fun. The adrenalin was flowing hard—I could feel it rising in me like mercury in a thermometer plunged in hot water—and by the end of the game I felt like a ghost. I was invisible. Invincible. I was so high there was no play I was incapable of making. It was as if the game had been a showcase for my talents.

The first batter hit a lazy two-hopper to me, the second batter did the same. The third walked. The clean-up hitter laced one straight up the middle, but I'd been shading him that way, and I back-handed the ball a good ten feet behind second base. If there had been no base runner it would have been an infield hit, but all I had to do was shovel the ball to Bobby Manuela, as he waited on the bag, like a tiger waiting for a steak, for the easy, inning-ending force-out.

I handled eight chances in all, my confidence growing with every one. I turned the pivot flawlessly on two double-play feeds from Manuela. The starting job was mine. I could play for fun, which I did.

And the fans! I have seldom heard such applause when I was introduced. I have *never* received such applause when I was introduced. Dilly Eastwick doubled as public-address announcer, sounding as if he were introducing the combatants in a heavy-weight boxing match.

"AND FROM CHICAGO, ILLINOIS . . ." he paused for a

fraction of a second to let the words echo, "VIA LOUISIANA STATE UNIVERSITY . . . OUR NEW SECOND-BASE MAN . . ." and again the fractional pause, "MIKE HOULE."

I was pleased to see he got the pronunciation right: Hool. In the Doll House Café I'd heard my name pronounced Hoo-lee, and Hoo-LAY, and someone even tried out HOW-lee.

The stands steadily filled as we took batting and infield practice. By the time the national anthem was sung, *a cappella,* by a grey-haired woman who was actually very good, the stands were packed and there were people standing and sitting on the grass in foul territory beyond the first- and third-base bleachers.

When we were at bat, besides studying the opposing pitcher I stared around the ballpark, wondering how an inter-squad game could generate such enthusiasm. The fans seemed evenly divided between the Greens and the Whites. Many of the fans behind our dugout wore white T-shirts with green trim, or actual white and green uniform tops and caps that matched ours. Some waved white pennants with green letters. The situation on the third-base side seemed identical except the color combinations were reversed. Someday there might be a civil war in Grand Mound: the Greens versus the Whites.

There was an aborted version of the wave practiced on both sides of the field, but each ended at mid grandstand, where I assume the fans for Green and fans for White divided. I was glad to see the wave fail. Like mascots, cheerleaders, and loud music it has no place in a thinking person's game like baseball. To me, the wave in baseball is the equivalent of cheering aloud at a chess match.

"What in the world do they do when the actual season begins?" I asked Bobby Manuela between innings, as we were refining our signals to be sure we always knew who would cover second in the event of a steal.

Bobby just smiled and shrugged. "They're a very expressive lot. That's why it's so much fun to play here."

"Are all the other towns in the league as baseball-mad as this one?"

"You'll see soon enough," said Bobby.

Vague answers are the norm here in Grand Mound. This morning, I asked Emmett, "What time does USA Today get to town, and where can I buy one?"

"Well, now, Mike," Emmett said, "we don't have much call for outside newspapers like that. Not that you can't get one," he added, noting my look of concern. "You can buy a copy of the Sunday Des Moines Register down at the drugstore, and I've heard they carry the Chicago Tribune some weekends. But, we have the Grand Mound Leader every day, and being off the beaten track as we are, we're more interested in what's happening in Grand Mound than anywhere else."

In the clubhouse after the game I met Dilly Eastwick, a round freckle-faced man who did not look like his voice.

"I'm Dilly Eastwick, the sports editor," he said, his small damp hand shaking mine. "I make a point of covering every Greenshirts game myself."

What I'd been expecting was a Babe Ruth with a journalism degree, someone large and craggy, who could still hit a home run in batting practice or silence a heckler with a fierce stare.

"Mike, I want you to know I really appreciated your play this evening. Why, you danced like Baryshnikov all around second base, and that back-handed stop in the seventh inning was one of the finest plays I've ever seen."

"Thank you very much, Mr. Eastwick," I said. The back-handed stop *had* been something. The go-ahead run was on second and would have scored easily if the ball had made it through the infield. I launched myself after it, sailing through the air, landing, glove hand outstretched, in time to smother the ball. There was no play, but it held the run at third, and the next batter popped out to end the inning.

"Oh, don't thank me. It was a perfect pleasure to watch you play baseball tonight. And to watch you run the bases." His eyes twinkled and his round, moon face beamed.

In addition to acquitting myself well in the field, I went two for four at the plate, with a sacrifice bunt, and stole three bases.

"Well, it's nice to be appreciated," I said.

"We're real special baseball fans here. You'll always be appreciated in Grand Mound, Mike. You can count on it. Now, if you'll excuse me I want to get a word with Dan Morgenstern. He's quite a catcher. That boy was throwing clotheslines to second base tonight."

The line about me dancing like Baryshnikov appeared in the next morning's edition of the *Grand Mound Leader*. So did a comment on my speed, "Mike Houle is so fast on the base paths, it's rumored he's able to play tennis by himself."

One cannot help but be pleased with press like that.

THIRTEEN

My second day in Grand Mound is over and I've made several friends. The scrap of gossip I overheard is indeed true, one of our players *is* Asian. His name is Stanley Wood, and he is the first-base man for the Green team. He is over six feet tall, raw-boned, his long, brush-cut hair gleaming like quills. He is trying, with only moderate success, to cultivate a Fu Manchu mustache.

After our second inter-squad game, again played before a full house of fans ravenous for baseball, I gravitated toward Stanley Wood, wanting to compare our experiences so far.

"That home run you hit must have cleared the fence by forty feet," I said. "Any guesses on how far it travelled?"

"Thanks. Certainly over four hundred feet. But that's because us Asians have better peripheral vision than you white guys."

I assumed he was kidding, but his lines were delivered with a fierce scowl worthy of Ming the Merciless.

"Is that what they say?" I asked innocently.

"Only my team. Yours, being across the field, didn't have to be so discreet."

"Fair enough. Welcome to the Midwest. Anyone different is a bit of a curiosity here. You're probably the first Chinese person they've seen outside of a Chinese restaurant."

"Not Chinese. Taiwanese. Before my family emigrated from Taiwan a few years ago, I helped win two Little League World Championships."

The scowl broke into an ironic smile.

"In case you're unable to tell, I'm being inscrutable," said Stanley. "We Asians study inscrutability in pre-school. Now, go ahead, take your best shot at the Taiwanese Little League Champions."

"Is this the visible minority section?" Daniel Morgenstern had sidled up to us.

"I'm not sure I qualify," I replied. "All I can claim is a rumor that I might be one-sixteenth Black Hawk or Nez Percé."

"Close enough. You guys looked like you were having a serious conversation."

"Stanley here played for Taiwan when they won the Little League World Series, which as far as I can tell could have been any year from 1960 to the present. I was just about to question the integrity of his accomplishment."

"Fine with me," said Daniel. "Tell us the truth now, how old were you guys, and how did you fool all the officials? I've seen players yanked off American Little League teams when their birthdate was one day out of line, but I bet some of the Taiwanese players had wives and children of their own."

"You exaggerate greatly, of course; I can assure you none of us were over eighteen," Stanley Wood said with a straight face. "Well, not many of us." Like a comedian, he paused for laughter. "As for documentation," he went on, "it is very easy to confuse such volatile things as birthdates when all computation is done with an abacus."

"Volatile?" said Daniel. "Is your birthday volatile, Mike?" He laughed. "I see we're not gonna get anywhere here. Seriously, how are you guys being treated?"

"I'm doing fine," I said. "My family is a little over-zealous, especially where food is concerned. On the other hand, I can state with some certainty that I am being groomed as son-in-law material, pun intended, which is a little embarrassing."

I am definitely *not* potential son-in-law material," said Stanley. "My family, the Lindfors, are horrified. It apparently never occurred to anyone in Grand Mound that Stanley Wood, of San Francisco, California, would not be white. Did your family know they were getting you?" he asked Dan.

"Evidently. I don't think it's a coincidence that I'm living with the only Jewish family in town."

"At least they knew what they were getting," Stanley said. "No one, including the executives of the ball club, knew what they were getting when they signed me. I was a last-minute replacement for someone who decided to teach English in Japan. My wily agent, Justin Birdsong, just didn't tell them."

"Justin Birdsong is your agent, too?" I asked.

"He must be a busy guy. He's mine, also," said Dan Morgenstern.

"You should have seen the face on that Dilly Eastwick character when Mr. Lindfors dragged me into the newspaper office. I guess he wanted Eastwick to see for himself. What a difference a *d* makes." And he smiled delightedly, showing wide spaces between his front teeth.

"So, how *did* you get a name like Wood?" Dan asked.

"My father, who, incidentally, is horrified that I am wasting my time playing baseball, when he moved his land development company to San Francisco, felt the name Woo was too obvious, and that if he added a *d*, business associates wouldn't find out we were Asian until they had to look us in the eye, so to speak."

"It appears to have worked too well," I said.

"I don't know about you guys, but I'm not getting any pressure to date or marry the Lindfors' darling daughter, which, ironically, I wouldn't mind doing. She's very pretty."

"I think you've discovered the secret to getting along in Grand Mound," said Daniel.

"Have Oriental features?" said Stanley.

"No. I was thinking maybe if Mike and I each add a letter to our name, it might work as a talisman to keep unwanted women at bay."

"What unwanted women?" I asked. "That's an oxymoron."

We experimented for a while at adding letters to our names.

We laughed and slapped each other on the back, getting sillier by the minute. There was an exhilaration in letting down after a tough game, as well as the tension of being in a new and odd situation.

"Does anyone have a car?" I asked. "I'd like to take in some of the surrounding towns, maybe drive down to Iowa City. University is still in session there, which means about fifteen thousand women to choose from. How about it?"

"I don't have a car," said Stanley.

"Me either," said Daniel. "They insisted we fly in, remember? I asked about driving down from New Jersey, but they preferred we didn't have cars."

"No one said that to me," I said. "How about a rental?"

"There's no car rental place in town," said Stanley. "We'd probably have to go to Cedar Rapids Airport."

"Catch-22," I said. "We need a car to get to Cedar Rapids."

"We could always have a Coke at the Doll House," said Daniel.

"If we can get past our families," I said. "Mine will be waiting for me."

"Mine won't," said Stanley Wood.

We settled for walking to the Doll House, though we had to turn down rides from both the Powells and the Greenspans. The Lindfors were nowhere to be seen. But as we were seating ourselves at the Doll House, the waitress Nan Hurchubise approached the table. She was wearing a yellow uniform that showed off her long legs and waist-length dark hair. Stanley stopped what he was saying in mid sentence, and a look passed between them. I caught it, but Daniel didn't.

"What pitch did you hit over the fence?" Daniel said to Stanley.

"A high, hard mistake," said Stanley.

Before we left the Doll House that night, Stanley had arranged a date with Nan for after the café closed.

FOURTEEN

Four of us newcomers—Stanley, Daniel, me, and the new pitcher, Crease Fowler—did manage an evening out. I was the instigator. I told Emmett that we wanted some time to do what young ballplayers usually did—I didn't specify shoot the breeze, enjoy a few beers, and look for female company. Emmett pulled in his cheeks and narrowed his eyes but didn't raise any objections. We decided intentionally not to include the fifth newcomer, Barry McMartin, in our evening out. Barry is a huge outfielder from Oklahoma with the build and blond good looks of a young Mickey Mantle, but he is a jerk: loud, crude, boisterous, and none of us wanted him along.

The evening didn't meet my expectations. Grand Mound night life is even less exciting than watching paint dry. We walked to Big Al's, a bar on the outskirts of town. Big Al's sounded interesting, but it was a dark place housed in an arched metal building, the type that usually holds machine shops and farm-equipment repair businesses. A blue neon Bud sign bled down the only window. Inside there was a long bar and two dozen tables, a juke box and a small dance floor that didn't look like it had been used this decade. There were a few farmers at the tables and along the bar, three young guys who looked like construction workers. The juke box wailed George Strait and Waylon Jennings. The biggest disappointment was that there were no women in the place. The bartender, a huge man with a walrus mustache and a beer gut, didn't wait tables. Customers walked to the bar, paid for their order, and carried their drinks back to their tables.

After an hour, a couple of women did come in, but they were thirty-something types, one in stretch pants and a University of Iowa sweat shirt, the other covered in a garish orange shawl.

"Somewhere there's a Winnebago without drapes," whispered Dan.

They took a table nearby and an interest in us. One of them tried to drag Crease to the muddy-looking dance floor, but he escaped. They turned their attention to the construction workers, who were a little closer to their age anyway.

We did get to talking about our past baseball lives. I told about my religious fanatic coaches in the South. Stanley told about playing on the Little League World Champions. Then Crease told us about his last stop before Grand Mound:

"My baseball career ended on a Tuesday night last August at the exact moment that Manny Embarquadero killed the general manager's dog. In a season scheduled to end August 31, Manny had arrived July 15, supposedly the organization's hottest prospect, an import from a tropical island where the gross national product is revolution, and the per capita income $77 a year. A place where, it is rumored, either heredity or a diet heavy in papaya juice causes young men to move with the agility of panthers and enables them to throw a baseball from Denver to Santa Fe on only one hop.

"According to what I had read in USA Today, there were only two political factions in Courteguay—the government and the insurgents—their titles depending on which one was currently in power. One of the current insurgents was a scout for our organization, reportedly receiving payment in hand grenades and flame-throwers. He spotted Manny Embarquadero in an isolated mountain village (on Manny's island, a mountain is anything more than fifteen feet above sea level) playing shortstop barefoot, fielding a pseudo-baseball supposedly made from a bull's scrotum stuffed with papaya seeds.

"Even a semi-competent player would have been an improvement over our shortstop, who was batting .211 and was always late covering second base on double-play balls.

"'The organization's sending us a phenom,' Dave 'The Deer' Dearly told us a few days before Manny's arrival. Dearly was a competent manager, pleasant and laid-back with his players. He knew a lot about baseball and was able to impart that knowledge, but on the field during a game, he was something else.

"'Been swallowing Ty Cobb Meanness Pills,' was how Mo Chadwick, our center fielder, described him. Dearly was developing a reputation as an umpire-baiting bastard, who flew off the handle at a called third strike, screamed like a rock singer, kicked dirt on umpires, punted his cap, and heaved water coolers onto the field with little or no provocation.

"'Got to have a gimmick,' he said out of the side of his mouth one night on the road, as he strutted back to the dugout after arguing a play where a dim-witted pinch runner had been out by thirty feet trying to steal third with two out. Dearly had screamed like a banshee, backed the umpire half way to the left-field foul pole, and closed out the protest by punting his cap into the third row behind our dugout. The fans loved to boo him.

"Before Manny Embarquadero arrived, my guess was that Dave Dearly would be the only one on the squad to make the Bigs.

"I planned on quitting organized baseball at the end of the season. My fastball was too slow and didn't have enough action; my curve was good when it found the strike zone, which wasn't often enough. I was being relegated to middle relief way down in A ball—not a positive situation.

"I agreed with Dearly that unless you were Roger Clemens or Griffey Jr, you needed a gimmick. As it turned out, Manny Embarquadero had a gimmick. If the ball club hadn't been so cheap that we had to bunk two to a room on the road, I never would have found out what it was.

"Manny looked like all the rest of those tropical paradise ballplayers, a polished black skin, head covered in a mass of wet black curls, thin as if he'd only eaten one meal a day all his life, thoroughbred legs, long fingers, buttermilk eyes.

"The day Manny arrived, the general manager, Chuck Manion, made a rare appearance in the clubhouse to introduce the hot new prospect.

"'Want you boys to take good care of Manny here. Make him feel welcome.

"Manny was standing, head bowed, dressed in ghetto-Goodwill-store style: black dress shoes, cheap black slacks, and a purple pimp-shirt with most of the glitter worn off.

"'Manny not only doesn't speak English,' Chuck Manion announced, 'he doesn't speak anything. He's mute, but not deaf. He knows no English or Spanish, but follows general instructions in basic sign language.

"'The amazing thing is he's hardly played baseball at all. He was able to communicate to our scout that he was seventeen years old and had never played competitive baseball. He truly is a natural. I've seen video tapes. The plays he makes on one month's experience, he'll be in the Bigs after spring training next year.'

"Chuck Manion was a jerk, about forty, a blond, red-faced guy who looked as if he had just stepped out of a barber's chair, even at eleven o'clock at night. Any time he came to the club-house, he wore a four-hundred-dollar monogrammed jogging suit and smelled of fifty-dollar-an-ounce aftershave. His family owned a brewery—and our team. Chuck Manion played at being general manager just for fun.

"'I bet he thought he'd get laid a lot, was why he wanted a baseball team as a toy,' said Mo Chadwick one night when Manion, playing the benevolent, slumming employer, accompanied a bunch of us players to a bar after a game. He seemed extremely disappointed that there weren't dozens of women in various stages of undress and sexual frustration crawling all over. 'Sucker thought he'd buy one round of drinks and catch the overflow.'

"He was right. Manion hung around just long enough for one drink and a few pointed questions about Baseball Sadies. As soon as he discovered that minor-league ballplayers didn't have to beat off sex-crazed groupies, he vanished into the night.

"'Going down to the airport strip to cruise for hookers in his big BMW,'" said Mo. Again I had to agree.

"After we all shook hands with Manny Embarquadero and patted him on the shoulder and welcomed him to the club, Manion made an announcement.

"'We're gonna make Crease here'—he placed a hand on my shoulder—'Manny's roommate both at home and on the road. Crease reads all the time so he won't mind that Manny isn't much of a conversationalist.' Manion laughed at his own joke.

"I did read some. In fact, I'd been involved in a real brouhaha with my coaches because I read on the bench and in the bullpen until my dubious expertise was needed on the mound. The coaches insisted that reading would ruin my control. I read anyway. I was threatened with unconditional release. I learned to hide my book more carefully. I notice that here in Grand Mound they don't care that I read in the bullpen, heck, a couple of other guys read too.

"My nickname, 'Crease,' by the way, came about because ever since Little League I'd creased the bill of my cap right down the middle until it was ridged like a roof above my face. I always imagined I could draw a straight line from the V in the bill of my cap to the catcher's mitt.

"'This guy is too good to be true,' Mo Chadwick said to me after we'd watched Manny Embarquadero work out. 'Something's not right. If he's only played baseball for one month, how come he knows when to back up third base, and how come he knows which way to cheat when the pitcher's going to throw off-speed?'

"'Ours is not to reason why,' I said. 'He's certainly a rough diamond.'

"If Manny Embarquadero hadn't talked in his sleep, I never

would have found out what a rough diamond he really was.

"Our first night together, I woke up in humid blackness on a sagging bed to the sound of loud whispering. The team had reserved the whole second floor of a very old hotel, so at first I assumed the sounds were in the hallway. But as I became wider awake, I realized the whispering was coming from the next bed.

"No one was certain what language, if any, Manny understood.

"'Our scout says he may understand some of the pidgin dialects from Courteguay,' Chuck Manion had said the day he introduced Manny. The mountains Manny had wandered out of bordered on Haiti, so there was some speculation that Manny might understand French. Needless to say there were no French-speaking players on the team.

"I raised the tattered blind a few inches to let a little street light into the room, just enough to determine that Manny was alone in bed. What I was hearing was indeed coming from his mouth, but it wasn't Spanish, or French, or even some mysterious Courteguayan dialect. It was ghetto American, inner-city street talk pure and simple, and I recognized it right away because I'm a Canadian, from Tecumseh, Ontario, not far from Windsor, which is connected by bridge to Detroit.

"He mumbled a lot, but also spoke several understandable phrases, as well as the words *Mothah*, and *Dude*, and *Dee-troit*. At one point he said clearly, 'Go ahead girl, it ain't gonna bite you.'

"At breakfast in the hotel coffee shop, Manny, using hand signals and facial expressions, let me know he wanted the same breakfast I was having: eggs, toast, hash browns, large orange juice, large milk, large coffee.

"'I think we should have a talk,' I said to Manny as soon as we got back to the room after breakfast.

"Manny stared at me, his face calm, his eyes defiant.

"'You talk in your sleep,' I said. 'Don't worry, I'm not going to tell anyone, at least not yet. But I think you'd better clue me in on what's going down.'

"Manny stared a long time, his black-bullet pupils boring right into me, as if he was considering doing me some irreparable physical damage.

"'If I was back home, mon, that stare would have shrivelled your brain to the size of a pea,' Manny said in a sing-songy Caribbean dialect.

"'Your home, from what I heard, is in Detroit,' I said, 'somewhere with a close-up view of the Renaissance Center. So don't give me this island peasant shit. When I look closely I can tell you're no more seventeen than I am. You're older than me, and I just turned twenty-three. I don't know why you're running this scam, and I don't particularly care. But if we're gonna room together you're gonna have to play it straight with me.'

"'Fuck! Why couldn't I draw a roomie who's a heavy sleeper? I really thought I'd trained myself to stop talking in my sleep.'

"The accent was pure inner-city Detroit, words flying past me like debris in the wind.

"'So, what's the scam? Why a mute, hot-shot, child prodigy of a shortstop from the hills of Courteguay?'

"'I just want to play baseball.'

"'That's no explanation.'

"'Yes, it is. I played high-school ball. I didn't get any invites to play for a college. I went to every tryout camp in the country for three years. Never got a tumble. "You're too slow. You don't

115

hit for power. Your arm is strong, but you don't have enough range." If you ain't the most talented then you got to play the angles. I seen that all the shortstops were coming from Courteguay, and they're black, and I'm black, so I figured if I went over there and kept my mouth shut and pretended to be an inexperienced kid from the outback, I'd get me a chance to play.'

"'But in a month or so, when you don't improve fast enough, this team is going to send you packing back to Courteguay.'

"'I'm gettin' better every day, man. I'm gonna make it. People perform according to expectations. Everyone figures I'll play my way into the Bigs next spring, and I'm not gonna disappoint them.'

"'There's a little matter of talent.'

"'I have more than you can imagine.'

"'Lots of luck.'

"The next night, the play-by-play people mentioned that Manny was mute but not deaf. By the eighth inning, there were a dozen people behind our dugout shouting to Manny in every language from Portuguese to Indonesian. Manny shrugged and smiled, displaying a faceful of large, white teeth.

"He was a 100-percent improvement on our previous short-stop. I could see what the scouts, believing him to be seventeen and inexperienced, had seen in him. He had an arm that wouldn't quit. He could go deep in the hole to spear a ball on the edge of the outfield grass, straighten effortlessly, brace his back foot on the grass, and fire a rocket to first in time to get the runner. He covered only as much ground as was necessary in order to reach the ball.

"Of course, his name wasn't Manny Embarquadero.

"'I am one anonymous dude. Jimmy, with two *m*'s, if you must know, Williams with two *l*'s. Hell, there must be two thousand guys in Dee-troit, Michigan, with the same name. And all us young black guys look alike, right?

"'I had a gramma, probably my greatgramma, but she died. I think I was her granddaughter's kid. But that girl went off to North Carolina when I was just a baby and nobody ever once heard from her. One time, Gramma and I lived for three years in an abandoned building. We collected cardboard boxes and made the walls about two feet thick. It gets fucking cold in Dee-troit, Michigan. Gramma always saw to it that I went to school.'

"Two nights later, there was a scout from the Big Show in the stands. Everyone pressed a little, some pressed a lot, and everybody except Manny looked bad at one time or another. Manny was unbelievable. One ball was hit sharply to his right and deep in the hole, a single if there ever was one. The left fielder had already run in about five steps, expecting to field the grounder, when he saw that Manny had not only fielded the ball, but was directly behind it when he scooped it up and threw the runner out by a step. What he did was humanly impossible.

"'How did you do that?' I asked, as he flopped down on the bench beside me after the inning. Manny just smiled and pounded his right fist into his left palm.

"Later, back at the hotel, I said, 'There was something fishy about that play you made in the sixth inning.'

"'What fishy?'

"'You moved about three long strides to your right and managed to get directly behind a ball that was hit like lightning. No major-league shortstop could have gotten to that ball. You're not a magician, are you?'

117

"'I'm not anything but a shortstop, man.' But he looked at me for a long time, and there was a shrewdness in his stare.

"What I could not understand was that no one else had noticed that one second he was starting a move to his right to snag a sure base hit, and an instant later he was behind the ball, playing it like a routine grounder. When I carefully broached the subject, no one showed any interest. He had not even been overwhelmed by congratulations when he came in from the field.

"I admired his audacity. It troubled me that on one of my many visits to Detroit to see the Tigers, the Pistons, or the Red Wings, I may have passed Manny/Jimmy on the street, in one of those groups of shouting, pushing, swivel-jointed young men who congregated outside the Detroit sports facilities.

"The trouble between Chuck Manion and Manny Embarquadero began on a hot Saturday afternoon, before a twilight doubleheader. Chuck Manion, wearing a sweat suit worth more than I was getting paid every month, showed up to work out with the team. He was accompanied by his dog, a nasty spotted terrier of some kind, with mean, watery eyes and a red ass. Manion sometimes left the dog in the clubhouse during a game, where it invariably relieved itself on the floor.

"'After losing in extra innings, it's a fucking joy to come back to a clubhouse that smells of dog shit,' The Deer said one evening.

"'Tell him where to stuff his ugly dog,' one of the players suggested. We all applauded.

"'Wouldn't I love to,' said Dearly. 'Unfortunately, Manion's family actually puts their own money into this club. An owner like that can do no wrong.'

"On that humid Saturday afternoon, Manion brought the

dog out onto the playing field. Dearly spat contemptuously as he hit out fungoes, but said nothing.

"Manny and I were tossing the ball on the sidelines, when Manion pointed to Manny and said to me, 'Tell Chico to take Conan here for a couple of turns around the outfield.'

"'His name is Manny,' I said. 'And he can understand simple sign language. Tell him yourself.'

"'You're the one who's retiring end of the season, aren't you?' Manion asked me in a snarky voice.

"'Right.'

"'And a goddamned good thing.'

"He walked over to Manny, put the leash in his hand, and pointed to the outfield, indicating two circles around it.

"I wondered what Manny Embarquadero would do. I *knew* what Jimmy Williams would do. But which one was Manion dealing with?

"It didn't take long to find out.

'Manny Embarquadero let the leash drop to the grass, and gave Manion the finger, staring at him with as much contempt as I had ever seen pass from one person to another.

"Manion snarled at Manny and turned away to hunt down Dave Dearly. At the same moment, Conan nipped at Manny's ankle.

"Manny's reaction was so immediate I didn't see it. But I heard the yelp, and saw the dog fly about fifteen feet into left field, his leash trailing after him.

"Manion found Dave Dearly, and demanded that Manny be fired, traded, deported, or arrested.

"'Goddamnit, Chuck,' Dearly responded, 'I got enough trouble babysitting and handholding twenty-five players, most of them rookies, without having you and your goddamned mutt riling things up.'

"The mutt, apparently undamaged, was relieving himself on the left-field grass, baring his pearly fangs at any ballplayer who got too close.

"Manion continued to froth at the mouth, threatening Dearly with unemployment if he didn't comply.

"At that moment, Dearly must have remembered his reputation as an umpire-baiter. His face turned stop-sign red as he breathed his fury onto Chuck Manion, backing him step by step from third base to the outfield, scuffing dirt on Manion's custom jogging outfit. Manion had only anger on his side.

"'Take your ugly fucking dog and get the fuck off my baseball field,' roared Dearly, turning away from Manion as suddenly as he had confronted him. Dearly punted his cap six rows into the empty stands, where it landed right side up, sitting like a white gull on a green grandstand seat.

"Manion retrieved the dog's leash and headed for the dugout, still raging and finger-pointing.

"'From now on, walk your own fucking dog on your own fucking lawn,' were Dearly's parting words as Manion's back retreated down the tunnel to the dressing room.

"The players applauded.

"'Way to go, Skip.'

"'You better watch out,' I said to Manny, after a late supper at a Jack-in-the-Box. 'Manion's gonna get your ass one way or another.'

"'Fuck Manion and his ball club,' said Manny Embarquadero. 'And fuck his dog, too.'

"Manion didn't show his face on the field all the next week, but he could be seen in the owner's box, a glass wall separating him from the press table, pacing, smoking, often taking or making phone calls.

"Manny continued his extraordinary play.

"'Did you see what I did there in the second inning?' Manny asked in our room after a game.

"'I did.'

"'I can't figure out how I did it. If anybody but you sees . . . what would they do, bar me from the game?'

"In the second inning, Manny Embarquadero had gone up the ladder for a line drive. The ball was far over his head, but I saw a long, licorice-colored arm extend maybe four feet farther than it should have. No one else, it seemed, saw the supernatural extension of the arm. They apparently saw only a very good play.

"'Want to tell me how you do what you do?' I said.

"Manny had made at least one impossible play in each of the last dozen games. At the plate it was less obvious, but probably magically inspired as well. He was batting over .400.

"'Must be because you know who I really am that you can see what I do,' said Manny. 'Besides, no one would believe you; I'm just a poor, mute, black, immigrant ballplayer.'

"'I've no intention of spreading your secret around. I'm going to be through with professional baseball in a few weeks. I don't enjoy the game that much. And I don't come through in the clutch.'

"'If you want a professional career, I might be able to arrange it. It would involve a trip to Courteguay. And I don't know, you being white and all.'

"'Not interested.'

"'There's a factory down there. They sing and chant over your body, wrap it in palm fronds, feed you hibiscus petals and lots of other things. After a week or so, you emerge from the factory with an iron arm, the speed of a bullet, and the ability to be in more than one place at a time.

"'It's just like a magic trick, only the whole ballplayer is quicker than the eye. They send a couple of guys up to the Bigs each year. I just lucked out. I really thought I'd stand a chance of getting a professional contract if I pretended to come from a backwater like Courteguay. The reason I got into the factory, got the treatment, was that I got caught stealing food that supposedly belonged to the leader of the insurgents, Dr. Noir. Looks like Idi Amin, only not so friendly . . .'

"'What do you have to do in return?'

"'You don't want to know,' said Manny.

"'Probably not. You're kidding me, right? There's no factory in Courteguay that turns out iron-armed infielders.'

"'Think whatever you want, man. This Dr. Noir was from Haiti: voodoo, dancing naked all night, cutting out people's spleens and eating them raw. Someday soon, Dr. Noir will be president of Courteguay again.'

"'You're right,' I said. 'I don't want to know.'

"A week later, after a short road trip, Dave Dearly was fired. We were in first place by a game, thanks mainly to Manny Embarquadero's fielding and hitting.

"The grapevine reported that Chuck Manion had been unable to convince the parent club to get rid of Manny. Dave Dearly was another matter. Since Manion and his family put large sums of money into the stadium and the team, the top kicks decided that if keeping him happy meant jettisoning a minor-league manager, so be it. The third-base coach, a young guy named Wylie Keene, managed the club the next night.

"'It was because The Deer went to bat for your Courteguayan friend over there,' Keene told me. 'Chuck Manion wanted Manny given the bum's rush out of baseball. But The Deer stood up for him.

"'He told the parent club that he wouldn't have his players treated that way, and that life was too short to work for an asshole like Manion. But, we all know money is the bottom line, so The Deer is gone. He thinks the organization will find another place for him.'

"'What do you think?'

"'I don't know. He's a good man. He'll catch on somewhere, but not likely in this organization.'

"When we got home I passed all that information to Manny.

"'Manion's a son-of-a-bitch,' Manny said. 'I'd love to get him to Courteguay for a few minutes. I'd like to leave him alone in a room with Dr. Noir. Hey, he's got a degree in chiropractics from a school in Davenport, Iowa. Dr. Lucius Noir. I saw his diploma. According to rumors, he deals personally with political prisoners. Dislocates joints until they confess to whatever he wants them to confess to. Wouldn't I love to hear Manion scream?'

"'Look, you're gonna be out of this town in just a couple of weeks. You'll never have to see Manion again.'

"'But there's something I have to do. Come on,' he said, heading for the door.

"'It's after midnight.'

"'Right.'

"We walked the darkened streets for over half an hour.

Manion's house overlooked the eighteenth tee of a private golf course. It looked like a mountain in the darkness.

"'Listen,' I said. 'I'm not going to let you do something you'll be sorry for, or get arrested for . . .'

"'Don't worry, I'm not going to touch him. The only way you can hurt rich people is by taking things away from them.'

"We crawled through a hedge and were creeping across Manion's patio when Conan came sniffing around the corner of the house. He stopped abruptly and stood stiff-legged, fangs bared, a growl deep in his throat.

"'Pretty doggy,' said Manny Embarquadero, holding a hand out toward the hairless, red-assed mutt. They stood like that for some time, until the dog decided to relax.

"Manny struck like a cobra. The dog was dead before it could utter a sound.

"'I should have killed Manion. But I got places to go.'

"'Somebody's gonna find out.'

"'How? Are you gonna tell? In Courteguay they'd barbecue that little fucker. There, dogs are a delicacy'

"'You're not from Courteguay'

"Manny was going to get caught. There was no doubt in my mind. He was going to ruin a promising baseball career, which may or may not have been aided by the supernatural. Personally, I had my doubts about Manny's stories, but I admired his chutzpah, his fearlessness.

"'Manny Embarquadero is pure magic. They'll never lay a hand on me,' said Jimmy Williams from Detroit, Michigan.

"'You forget,' I said, 'there isn't anyone named Manny Embarquadero.'

"'Oh, yes, there is,' he said. 'Oh, yes, there is.'

"As we crawled through the hedge, I let a branch take the creased cap off my head. A bus passed through town at 4:00 A.M., and I'd be on it."

"So," I asked Crease, "how did you end up in Grand Mound?"

"I'm not sure why they called me. They must have seen something in me that no one else had. Or else I got one hell of a recommendation from Chuck Manion. It was Dilly Eastwick who called Justin Birdsong and told him I would fit in perfectly in Grand Mound."

FIFTEEN

On the third evening the game went fifteen innings, and I actually produced in the clutch. In the bottom of the fifteenth, with a runner on first, I hit to the opposite field, a solid grounder through the right side, behind the runner, sending him easily to third. He scored the winning run on a sacrifice fly.

I know it sounds odd, but playing here is like playing a pickup game when I was a kid. The only difference is two of my fantasies have been fulfilled. We have a stadium full of fans and our own uniforms.

After the extra-inning win, my family and the Greenspans were chatting when Stanley, Daniel, and I walked out to the parking lot.

"On guard, guys," said Stanley, out of the side of his mouth, "they're planning a double wedding."

No one was waiting for Stanley, but he was anxious to head for the Doll House.

Tracy Ellen quickly pulled me aside.

"Walk me home, Mike. There's something I want to talk to you about." We eased away from the group.

"You kids have fun," Emmett said, grinning like the Cheshire Cat.

It was magic time, that special few minutes before sunset when the sky is at its most spectacular, when light has such special properties that it makes the dreams of moviemakers come true. Byron and I were extras in a movie one summer. The filming was on a farm a couple of miles into the country. We rode our bikes out to the set for three consecutive days and sat around for hours waiting for the magic time so we and fifty other kids could run screaming from the woods as if something was chasing us.

As Tracy Ellen and I made our way slowly down the main street of Grand Mound, and began climbing toward the ridge where the Powell's house stood, the sky behind the ridge was a vibrant raspberry. It looked as if it had been papered with hollyhock petals. Shadows of trees and houses were long and black, like pen-and-ink drawings.

"I thought we should straighten out a few things," Tracy Ellen said. "To start with, I should apologize for my parents. I can't believe how pushy they are. They are so obvious. Or at least my dad is. He has no sense of shame. When you're around, Mom at least pretends to be horrified by the way Dad pushes us together, but she's just as conniving as he is."

At supper the night before, Emmett had been more lavish than usual in his praise of Tracy Ellen's cooking, and Tracy Ellen in general.

"I understand what your parents are trying to do," I said. "I'm certain they mean well."

We passed Powell Real Estate and Insurance. There were a half-dozen cars parked across the street in front of the Doll House Café.

I kept glancing at Tracy Ellen as we walked along, wondering how I felt about her; I wondered how I *could* feel about her if given the chance. The sunset touched her pale hair, turning it red-golden. She was wearing a peach-colored blouse, faded jeans, and low cut black boots with ornamental silver buckles. I was very tempted to reach over and take her hand. Perhaps Emmett Powell knew what he was doing after all.

"I know what my folks are doing must annoy you a lot. So, if it will take some of the pressure off, you should know I have a boyfriend," said Tracy Ellen, bringing my fantasies to a crashing halt.

I felt more than a tiny tinge of sadness at the announcement. I suppose I'd hoped . . .

"They're pushing us together so hard I pretty well have to have a boyfriend."

Was her voice tinged with sadness, too?

"But I think it would be nice if we could be friends," she continued. "My brothers are a lot older. I was just a little kid when they went off to college. They're both married with their own lives. Nick, he's the oldest, even has a baby daughter."

"I think having you for a friend would be great," I said. "I've never had a sister. It'll be fun."

Now that Tracy Ellen was suddenly unattainable, I was more attracted to her than I had been at any time since my arrival in Grand Mound. It was crazy. My heart was thumping. I felt real sadness.

"Do you know what a slug's favorite novel is? *Slime and Punishment*," I said suddenly. Apparently stupidly, for Tracy Ellen glanced at me as if I were demented. We walked on in silence.

"Maybe if you said something to Dad about not trying so hard to marry us off, he might listen."

"I'll try to be tactful," I said.

We walked the rest of the way in silence. By the time we reached the house, the sun had disappeared behind Grand Mound. Magic time was over.

When I did confront Emmett, I wasn't very tactful.

"Tracy Ellen and I have made an agreement," I said, as we drove to work the next morning. "We're going to be friends, not sweethearts, so you can stop promoting a romance." Emmett, all innocence, glanced sideways at me over the top of his glasses.

"My dad always says the best policy is to let nature take its course. Don't try to help it along too much."

"My theory," said Emmett, "is that nature often needs a helping hand."

"Besides, Tracy Ellen tells me she already has a boyfriend."

"Oh, yes," said Emmett, his voice full of disapproval. "A boy from up around Mechanicsville. Built like a Clydesdale. And I might be doing a disservice to the horse to compare their intelligence."

"Sure you're not just being an over-protective father? Tracy Ellen strikes me as a pretty sensible girl."

"His name is Shag Wilson. He chews snuff. He drives a customized half-ton truck with tractor wheels about eight feet tall."

"You've made your point," I said.

And for the first time in my life I felt a painful twinge in my chest that I diagnosed as jealousy.

SIXTEEN

"I'm coming down for the weekend," my dad announced, when I called him later that evening. "I hate to admit it but I'm lonesome for you, and for a well-played baseball game."

"I told you, we're only playing inter-squad games. Season doesn't open for a couple of weeks."

"I'll take off work early Friday. See you after your game that evening. Knock in a couple of runs for me."

The next morning, in the *Grand Mound Leader* Dilly Eastwick compared my throws to first from the shortstop side of second and from deep on the right-field grass to a gunboat firing across the prow of a suspect ship. I cut the column out to show to Dad on his arrival.

In the following issue he tagged me with a nickname. Mike "Gunboat" Houle, the story said, effortlessly handled six chances in the field, and turned the pivot flawlessly on three double plays.

I was beginning to like Dilly Eastwick.

In the same issue, Dilly, as he insisted the players call him, wrote about Dan Morgenstern: "He fires clotheslines to second base, so straight and true that the flight path remains marked in the air for innings. You could hang the entire family wash on one of the throws of 'Clothesline' Morgenstern."

And so it went. Dilly is like an agent and press agent rolled into one. He nicknamed Stanley Wood the "Taiwanese Titan," and I've discovered almost every player on the team has a nickname, some more colorful and successful and descriptive than others.

After the story appeared fans immediately began calling me Gunboat, and requesting that my autographs be signed that way.

Clothesline Morgenstern's nickname also caught on, but I've yet to hear anyone address Stanley Wood as the Taiwanese Titan.

"He should have named me Burnham Wood," said Stanley, who in real life was an English major. "But then I don't suppose Dilly Eastwick has much time to read Shakespeare. It must consume all his waking hours coming up with nicknames for thirty-eight baseball players—and amateurs at that."

"Hey, speak for yourself," I said. "I turned down solid job offers from AT&T, IBM, and two brokerage houses to play here this summer. For me Grand Mound is a stepping stone to professional baseball."

"Right," said Stanley, his voice dripping sarcasm. "On the other hand, at least you have a career in finance to fall back on. As an English major, I need two more degrees to land a part-time job teaching bonehead English in some fourth-rate community college. My father is acquiring whole tracts of land in the Coachella Valley, outside Palm Springs, California. Perhaps I'm qualified to carry my old man's money to the bank, or maybe, if the Dodgers don't discover me this summer, I can landscape a couple of boring housing projects he's planning out in the desert."

"Doesn't your father want you by his side in the family business?"

"My father sees himself as an Asian Donald Trump. Anything I get I have to earn. Needless to say he is not thrilled that I am playing baseball instead of pursuing the Taiwanese Dream."

"How about you, Dan? You looking to play in the Bigs?"

"This is a pivotal summer for me. If I don't prove myself this summer, I have medical school staring me in the face come fall. I'm disappointed I wasn't drafted, but I'm also realistic enough to know that some of the greatest players were passed over in the draft. I'm not only a good player, I'm a great one—I've studied hours of tapes of Johnny Bench. I can make his every move behind the plate, and while I'm not as much of a power hitter I'm good enough to play ten years in the Bigs."

"That's what I like—ambivalence about your future," said Stanley.

"They've assured me that big-league scouts in the Midwest look in at the Cornbelt League every few weeks. I expect to be in Triple A by September," said Dan.

"When do they start making the cuts?" I wondered.

"I asked one of the veterans just this afternoon," said Stanley. "'Not for a few days yet,' he said. 'But there are so many players,' I said. 'Two full squads.'

"'Don't fret,' the guy said. 'Even after league play opens, they carry a very large roster.'"

"My goodness, where will he stay?" Marge Powell said when I told her my father was coming down from Chicago for the weekend.

"Isn't there a hotel or motel in Grand Mound?"

"There's no hotel. There's an older motel out on the highway, but I'm sure it isn't the kind of place your father would want to stay."

Does it have a roof, a floor, and a bed? I was tempted to reply. I could see my dad's stocky body, looking like an old sofa badly in need of new upholstery. When Byron and I were kids, Dad used to take us on vacation. We'd head off for no place in particular, traveling the back roads, stopping at mom-and-pop motels where the neon sign had long been dead and the painted signs had weathered pale and almost unreadable.

"If it has a roof, a floor, and a bed, I reckon it will do fine," Dad would say, as we stood in the tiny office of a faded motel, the cabins receding into the earth. But there was something about Dad and strangers. This big, gentle man, sad as a lost hound dog, rumpled as an unmade bed, trailing two boys, their dishevelled clothes advertising their motherless state, took only a matter of seconds to convince people of his harmlessness, his need.

Several times we ended up in the motel owner's kitchen, Dad drinking coffee, the wife feeding Byron and me, offering to bathe us, sometimes actually doing it, sending us to our room with a plateful of cookies, inviting us to breakfast in the morning.

In one place we stopped, the motel manager had been a barber; he ended up unwrapping his barber tools and giving all three of us haircuts, just because something Dad said reminded him of how much pleasure his former trade had brought to him.

"People are basically nice, you just have to give them a chance to show it," Dad would say.

Another time, we spent the night at a motel where a couple of the cabins were under renovation; it was somewhere in Missouri, the motel catered to parents visiting a girls college in a nearby town. Dad and the motel owner got to talking lumber, and Dad ended up pitching in on the work, while Byron and I spent our days gliding like fish in the small sun-heated swimming pool.

"We'll have to find someplace suitable for him to stay," Marge said, bringing me back to reality. "We'd have room if we hadn't converted one extra bedroom into a sewing room, and the other into an office for Emmett; as you've seen he ends up doing at least half his business from the house."

"Look, it's no problem. I'm sure there's a motel within a few miles that will be fine."

"I'll speak to Peggy McNee, next door," Marge went on, ignoring me. "Her house is small, but she has an extra bedroom."

I had only seen Mrs. McNee watering the flower beds in her yard. She was a middle-aged woman with reddish hair and a brisk walk when she headed across the lawn to her red Honda, which she kept parked at the curb. She sat on the first-base side at the ball games.

"I want you to come next door and look at the room Peggy McNee has for your father," Marge said at breakfast the next morning. "You can decide if it will be all right."

"Does it have a roof, a floor, and a bed?" I asked. "Those are Dad's criteria for overnight accommodation."

The second I finished my breakfast, Marge guided me next door. Mrs. McNee's home was a small white bungalow with green trim and green shutters. When she answered the door I saw she was younger than I'd thought, the word *widow* in my mind automatically meant age, though my own father had been a widower at twenty-five.

The inside of the house was immaculate. There was too much furniture, but it was relatively new and color-coordinated, in pastel blue and pink. Mrs. McNee had a married daughter in Cedar Rapids, and it was her former room that was proposed for my father.

I almost laughed aloud when I saw it. It was decorated in pink and white, with ruffled white curtains, and a pink and white canopy over the bed. There were satin pillows everywhere, a rocking chair with a knitted cushion, and crocheted and tatted doilies covered the chest of drawers, the table, and nightstand. Stuffed animals and dolls in formal dresses were strewn about with planned casualness.

"Do you think this will be all right, Mike?" Marge asked.

"My dad's a real nice man, but honestly this isn't his style. Mrs. McNee, how would you feel if someone dragged an automobile transmission into this room? My dad's likely to arrive wearing his work clothes, and well, I think he'd feel like a bull in a china shop."

"My late husband worked for Grand Mound Motors for many years," Mrs. McNee said. "I know all about automobile transmissions."

"It was a figure of speech," I said.

"It has a roof, a floor, and a bed," said Marge. "It will do fine."

My father rolled in at suppertime on Friday.

"I took a sick day," he said, hugging me and pounding my back heartily. "I was sick and tired of servicing and repairing fork lifts." He was wearing a jacket and slacks, his tie loose. He smelled of fresh-cut lumber and lime cologne.

"I haven't taken a sick day in seven years. And I told the lumberyard I was going to be sick on Monday, too. Monday is your day off, isn't it?"

"After noon. I have to work in the insurance office in the morning."

"Good enough."

Just by being himself my father charmed the Powells completely. He ate everything put in front of him and accepted seconds and thirds without complaint, which endeared him to Marge and Tracy Ellen.

When Emmett complimented him on raising two very young sons alone, Dad simply said, "I've been lucky. The boys have seldom given me a minute's grief."

"I'm sure luck had nothing to do with it," said Emmett.

"If we'd known you were arriving so early we'd have invited Peggy McNee to have dinner with us. We've arranged for you to use her guest room."

I'd told Dad on the phone that he would be staying next door, and that he was expected to pay regular motel rates. I also warned him that it was fancy.

"I don't want to put anybody out," Dad said.

Marge must have been busy on the phone, because Peggy McNee arrived shortly after dinner to accompany us to the baseball game, something she had never done before.

She was a beautiful woman. Her hair was a deep strawberry blonde, which accentuated sparkling blue eyes. She wore a long brown and yellow dress and a matching sun bonnet, which on some women would have looked ridiculous, but the outfit suited her, just as my dad's permanently rumpled look suited him.

They sat directly behind our dugout. As I came off the field at the end of the third, Dad stood to applaud a particularly good play I'd made to end the inning. He had to disengage his hand from Peggy McNee's. By the seventh they were much more interested in each other than the game.

My guess would be that Dad never even got to see the inside of the guest room at Peggy McNee's.

The next morning Dad was smiling so much it looked like his teeth had grown overnight.

On Saturday Peggy drove my dad all around the Grand Mound area; they took a picnic lunch and barely made it back in time for the game. Shortly after the game began, a cloud bank that had been assembling on the western horizon rolled in over Grand Mound and unleashed a deluge. The wind was huge, thrashing through the trees and rattling windows. Lightning created brilliant silver zippers across the clouds, which were several shades of black on black. The rain bedevilled roofs and overflowed gutters.

A good old-fashioned gully-washer, Emmett called it.

The game was canceled. Marge and Tracy Ellen baked cinnamon buns, and the six of us sat around the kitchen table drinking coffee and laughing as the rain tattooed on the windows.

If there is anything in the way of food more wonderful than fresh-baked cinnamon buns, I have yet to find it. The brown sugar, cinnamon, and butter had melded to the perfect consistency, the bread was light as an angel. As the rain abated, I imagined the smell of cooked cinnamon and sugar traveling across town through the rain-fresh air, attracting, like the Pied Piper, a crowd, a following, a mob anxious to share.

"The secret," Marge admitted, "is adding a few drops of vinegar to the bread dough."

I made a mental note of vinegar as secret ingredient in the world's best cinnamon buns. I planned to try the secret myself, and would certainly pass it along to my bride, when and if . . .

Dad and Peggy McNee didn't need two seats for the Sunday afternoon game. They cuddled like teenagers, feeding each other hot dogs, sharing sodas.

"I'd say your dad has found himself a girlfriend," Emmett said, looking for all the world like the proud matchmaker.

4

Barry McMartin

SEVENTEEN

Every Wednesday after the game we Powells—to Grand Mound it seems I am a Powell—stop at the Grand Mound Bowling Alley and Starlite Café for a few lines.

"We have to do what we can for the businesses in Grand Mound," said Emmett. "That's why we buy groceries at the Grand Mound Co-op, and why all the local people buy their insurance from me. By the way, Mike, do you know what it took for the young man to invest in long-term bonds? Maturity." We all groan appropriately while Emmett beams.

"I know you enjoy bowling, Mike," says Emmett.

"How would you know that?"

"Oh, I guess your agent must have mentioned it."

"I've never met my agent. We've never discussed anything but baseball and money."

I do like bowling. Dad dragged us to the lanes as soon as we were grown enough to bowl with both hands. I am about to try to pin Emmett down, find out where he is getting his information, when Tracy Ellen interrupts.

"Maybe you could help me," says Tracy Ellen. She is wearing a rose-colored blouse with a matching ribbon in her hair. "I seem to turn my wrist when I let go of the ball."

I want to say, 'Why don't you get a lesson from Shag Wilson? He gets to teach you about everything else." But that would be churlish and reflect more on my state of mind than on Shag Wilson's inappropriateness as a boyfriend for Tracy Ellen. I am jealous.

"I'd be happy to do what I can," I say. At least it's a chance to be close to Tracy Ellen. I show her how to keep her wrist straight. I line her up on the lanes, adjust her hips before each shot, straighten or slacken her posture. I want to turn her around to face me and kiss her ever so gently. Tracy Ellen seems oblivious to anything but bowling instruction, though Emmett is beaming, and makes a couple of, for him, mildly suggestive comments about the way I am handling his daughter. Tracy Ellen is a quick learner, and her score of 152 is, I'm told, her best ever.

Many of the bowlers had been at the baseball game, and I got ribbed good-naturedly about a slide I took to break up a double play in the eighth inning. I started my slide too soon, came up ten feet short of the bag, and was left there in a cloud of dust as the Green team completed the play and trotted off the field.

This is the night I get my first good look at Shag Wilson. Just as we're finishing up, he arrives to pick up Tracy Ellen. Even over the thunder of the bowling balls and pins I can hear the rumble of Shag's truck as he parks it in front of the glass doors to the bowling alley. He is short. He swaggers. He looks like something from a traveling company of *West Side Story*. He wears a tight white T-shirt, jeans, and motorcycle boots. He has full lips, short arms, and stubby hands. His tin of chew has worn a circle into the back right pocket of his jeans.

How can Tracy Ellen see anything in this guy? Maybe it's just that he is as unlike Emmett as it is possible to be. Probably that's it. In my experience, teenage girls are attracted to men the exact opposite of their fathers. Tracy Ellen gives us all a quick wave, and she's gone.

"Ah, young people," says Emmett. Then, "Say, Mike, you know what the loser of a lawsuit experiences? Lien times. Ha!"

There was a really ugly happening at the game last night. Bad sportsmanship has not been a problem in the days I've been here. The umpires, there are three of them, are the owner of the feed store, a farmer from west of town, and the baseball and football coach at Grand Mound High School.

In any baseball games there are close plays, there are plays where the call could go either way. There have been plays where it certainly looked to me as if the umpires were wrong. But there has been very little argument. Players question a called strike. The first-base coach disputes a bang-bang play at the bag. The manager or acting manager disputes a close play at the plate. The umpires allow a certain amount of protest, then signal firmly that the game is to continue, and players and management comply.

Suicide Walston gets in his two-cents worth when the occasion requires, in fact he managed to get thrown out of one game for protesting a third-strike call on Stanley Wood. The pitch was high and hard and Stanley ducked back, though his bat did approach the strike zone. The plate umpire, the farmer from west of town, called strike three, and the brouhaha was on.

It was apparent from where we were sitting that Stanley had not gone around. Since managers aren't allowed to protest ball or strike calls, Walston was thumbed from the game as soon as he charged toward the plate. He bellowed into the umpire's face for a minute or two, then left the field, stalking away angrily like a bantam rooster, snarling over his shoulder.

But what happened last night was entirely different.

The score was 3-1 in the eighth for the Green team. There was a man on first when Barry McMartin came to the plate. He slammed the first pitch deep into right-center field where neither outfielder could get to it; the ball rolled to the wall as the runners steamed around the bases. The right fielder did not pick the ball up cleanly, and the first runner scored easily.

I had one eye on Barry McMartin as I watched the throw from the outfield coming toward me. The third-base coach was trying to hold him up, but I could see McMartin planned on scoring, and it looked like he had a good chance. My throw to the catcher, who was blocking the plate, would have to be perfect.

I took the cut-off and threw a strike to the catcher, who tagged the sliding McMartin in a play that could have gone either way.

The umpire called McMartin out.

As the dust was still rising, McMartin came up roaring and flailing, his cheeks scarlet, his eyes bugging from his head. The runner who had scored in front of him, an outfielder named Lee Harwood, had been just off home plate, crouching, signalling McMartin to slide. Lee virtually leapt on McMartin's shoulders as he backed the somewhat surprised umpire toward the backstop.

Like slapping a mosquito, McMartin smashed Lee off his back, the surprised outfielder landing like a bag full of bats, stunned, his cheek already swelling where McMartin had struck him.

Gene Walston, who was coaching the Green team, and Vince Singletary, who was coaching us, both sprinted toward the plate, arriving about the time McMartin, screaming like a banshee, bumped solidly into the umpire, not knocking him off his feet, but sending him staggering into the screen, which allowed him to keep his balance.

Walston was screaming at McMartin to cool down, while Singletary was trying to get hold of McMartin; but McMartin was agile, and Singletary, even at close to three hundred pounds, couldn't quite hold him.

McMartin was now completely berserk. Walston jumped on his back, and was tossed off as if he'd been riding a bucking bronco. The catcher threw a rolling block, hitting McMartin behind the knees and sending him sprawling in the dirt. Singletary dived for him but missed. McMartin was crawling on his hands and knees, still screaming, dragging the catcher, who had a solid grip on his left leg.

McMartin finally shook free, raced to his own dugout and hurled seven or eight bats in a shower of white ash toward the playing field. Then he used another bat to hold his own team, the managers, and the umpires at bay, swinging it in a wide, sweeping motion with his left hand, while with his right he would pitch a bat, rearing back like a spear chucker, sending it into the midst of those trying to reach him.

He tossed at least five bats, then turned his attention to the dugout. He went for the water cooler, swinging like he was trying to hit a home run. Fortunately, the water cooler was made of flexible plastic. All he managed to do was knock it off its stand. He whacked at the leaking cooler a few times, then picked it up over his head and tossed it all the way to third base.

He again armed himself with a bat, but we never found out

what his intentions were, for Vince Singletary and Roger Cash had circled around and gotten on top of the dugout while McMartin was inside. Just as he emerged, he was hit by over five hundred pounds of assistant coach and groundskeeper. Several other players joined in and McMartin was pinned solidly to the earth.

As the Green team rallied in the ninth to win the game 4-3, McMartin was locked in the back of the town's only patrol car, where he raged ineffectually for a good ten minutes before coming to his senses.

"I've never seen anything like that," said Emmett later, as we sat at the kitchen table eating pie. "I saw the films of Chuck Cottier, when he was managing Seattle, tossing bats and a water cooler on the field. But he was just displaying his anger. I'm sure he wasn't trying to kill anybody. What do you think, Mike? Was he trying to kill somebody?"

"He was completely out of control. If he hadn't been stopped, he certainly would have hurt someone."

"He has a history of this kind of thing," said Emmett. "We thought we knew how to handle him. That's why we decided to give him a final chance here in Grand Mound. But he hasn't responded the way we hoped. A snag in our plans."

"What plans?"

"Nothing to concern yourself with, Mike."

"No. Wait a minute. Am I responding the way you'd hoped?"

"An unfortunate choice of words, Mike," said Emmett. "We don't have any plans for anyone, other than seeing them play good baseball and enjoy their time in Grand Mound."

We didn't see Barry McMartin for the next two days. There were a lot of rumors making the rounds. Someone said he'd been driven to the Cedar Rapids Airport right after the game and put on the first available flight back to his home town in Oklahoma. Someone else said he'd been hauled off to the psych ward at the University of Iowa Hospital in Iowa City. Another rumor had it that he was under a sort of house arrest at the home of his family, the Millers, where a deputy sheriff was watching him twenty-four hours a day.

And those were the least bizarre rumors. Another player said he'd heard that Barry had beaten up Mr. Miller, stolen his car, and was last seen careening down Highway 30 at about a hundred miles an hour.

Suicide Walston and Vince Singletary weren't talking. It was as if Barry McMartin had disappeared from the face of the earth.

It was another inaccurate rumor that allowed me to hear the whole story. Two nights after the incident at Fred Noonan Field, as I was sitting in the living room with Emmett and Marge—Tracy Ellen was out with Shag Wilson—there was a knock at the front door.

Emmett, assuming it was a local wanting to insure something, answered, talked briefly, then signalled it was for me. He looked puzzled and somewhat dubious as he waved me toward the door.

Barry McMartin was standing on the front porch.

"What can I do for you?" I said.

"Mike, I've got to talk. You may be the only one who can help me."

"Help you? How?"

"One of the guys said you were a psych major, and I gotta talk to someone about my weird behavior. The only reason the Millers let me out of the house was I told them I was coming to talk with a guy who was going to be a psychiatrist."

"You got it all wrong," I said. "Business. I'm a business major. I can give you lots of advice if you want to open a Dairy Queen, or start a chinchilla farm in your basement. But I get all my psychology from watching Oprah."

I could see the disappointment on his face.

"Goddamn! I've got to talk to somebody. Are business majors good listeners?"

"I don't know."

"Let's go for a walk. Please, I want to hear my own voice for a while. Maybe if I talk some of this shit out, I'll be able to get a handle on my fife."

"Give me a minute," I said, and went back inside.

"I'm going for a walk with Barry McMartin," I said.

"Are you sure it's safe?" asked Emmett.

"I'm not gonna disagree with anything he says. I'm just gonna listen. The guy's obviously disturbed."

"That's what I worry about."

"I'll be okay"

EIGHTEEN

Barry and I walked down the hill toward the heart of town. The moon was full, a glorious illuminated grapefruit in the center of the sky.

"Sorry about the psych rumor," I said.

"You read a lot. Guess some of the guys mistook what you were studying."

"Where did you go to school?"

"Oklahoma," said Barry.

"What did you major in?"

"Dingers and broads, man. Half the time I didn't even know what courses I was in. Every course was pass/fail, which meant if you attended a couple of times a semester and didn't shit on the prof's desk, you got a pass.

"I took this course on Navajo pottery. The only thing we did other than look at picture books was we went to this museum, and the prof says, 'These are Navajo pots and everything else isn't.' And that was it, a pass. Five credits toward an interdisciplinary degree with an undeclared major. How about that! You know what the Arts grad said to the Business grad? 'Want fries with your burger?' That's why I've got to play baseball, Mike."

"Do you have any idea why you lose control the way you did?"

"Yeah, I do."

'Well, recognizing the problem is half the battle. At least that's what psych majors say"

"Mike, I came over to your place to open up to you, tell you things I've hardly even admitted to myself, let alone spoken aloud."

"And you still want to do that?"

"Hell, what have I got left to lose? Will you listen, Mike? Will you hear me out?"

I thought about it for a moment. I decided I can listen as well as the next guy.

'Tell me whatever you want," I said. "Strictly confidential."

We strolled through the downtown, the streets silent. We ended up at the ballpark, sitting in the stands, just to the outfield side of first base. The dew was beginning to fall and the odors of the ballpark at night filled our senses.

Barry McMartin talked.

"My buddies Pascoe and Martinez came to visit me at Vancouver General Hospital the day after I picked up forty-one stitches from running through the plate-glass wall next to the front door of my girlfriend's apartment building.

"Pascoe was black. He was our first-base man, in his third year in Triple A and not likely to go any higher, even for a cup of coffee. He was six foot seven and shaved his head to resemble a pro wrestler; he looked mean as a boil, but one of the reasons he was never going to get a shot at the Bigs was he lacked the killer instinct. He played an average first base, but for such a big man he had only warning-track power.

"Martinez was new to the team, came from the Dominican Republic, that famous town where they turn out iron-armed shortstops who gobble up ground balls as if they were part of a video game.

"Martinez spoke only about ten words of English, so he was happy to have anybody pay attention to him. He had worried brown eyes and was so black his round cheeks and wide forehead gave off a glare in bright sunlight. Martinez had no idea he was getting himself in the manager's bad books, making himself an outcast by hanging around with me. But Pascoe knew.

"Reporters described me as the team's designated flake. A bad boy who didn't have lights on in every room. A troublemaker. Most of my teammates disliked me and were a little afraid of me. Which I didn't mind.

"Some of them thought I was on drugs. Which I did mind. I never did drugs. Never will. I do have some common sense.

"At the hospital, Pascoe stuck his head around the door-jamb and said, 'McMartin, how the hell did you get all the way to Triple A on one damn brain cell?'

"I smiled, though it hurt like hell. Nine of those forty-one stitches were in my hairline. Martinez grinned, said something in Spanish, and ended by clapping his hands and doing a little dance step. I assumed he was wishing me well.

"'How long will you be out of action this time?' Pascoe asked.

"'Management put me on the fifteen-day disabled list. I'll be ready to go in less than that.'

"'You are very lucky you are not dead,' is what the doctor in emergency said to me as he was sewing up my cuts. 'A couple of guys get killed every month doing what you did tonight. You must have a guardian angel. You'll be back playing baseball in-side of two weeks.'

"I pulled up my hospital gown and showed the guys the rest of my stitches, like a primitive mark of Zorro on my chest. Not close to an artery, not even a tendon. What scared me at the time was a shard of glass clipped the tip off my right earlobe and I bled like a stuck pig. I came to lying in a pool of blood and glass. I thought I was a goner for sure.

"'Well, what are we gonna do to cheer our friend up, Marty?' Pascoe asked, with a smile that went halfway to his ears.

"'Si,' said Martinez.

"'Tell me a joke,' I said.

"'We know he can't play, Lady. We want to use him for sec-ond base,' said Pascoe, and we both broke up, while Martinez watched, mystified. My laughter lasted only a few seconds be-fore pain from my stitches brought me up short.

"One night early in the season, soon after I became Pascoe's roommate, we stayed up all night telling jokes. We were sitting in a twenty-four-hour café, and we just kept drinking coffee and telling stories until the sun came up. We told every joke we knew, clean or dirty.

"Gradually, instead of retelling a whole story, we'd just shout out the punchline. We both knew the joke so we could both laugh. Like, there's a long shaggy-dog story about a white man trying to prove himself to the Indian tribe he's living with. The Indians give him a list of acts to prove his courage. When he comes back to camp, looking happy but torn to rat shit, the chief says to him, 'You were supposed to kill the bear and make love to the woman.' So we'd just shout out the punchline and laugh like crazy. But it stymies players who aren't into storytelling, and doesn't go over well on dates.

"'The trouble was the pilot was gay,' I said, and this time Martinez laughed along.

"Martinez was so congenial we were teaching him real English, not the kind we taught to some of the Spanish-speaking players. We had been known to coach a Spanish player, at a restaurant, to say to the waitress, thinking he was ordering a hamburger, 'I would like to eat your pussy, please.'

"'What did management say?' Pascoe asked, changing the subject.

"'When you get to my balls try to act as if nothing unusual is happening,' I replied. That's a punchline from a joke about a famous detective going undercover in drag.

"'I'm serious,' said Pascoe.

"'So am I.'

"'Goddamnit, Barry. How much trouble are you in?'

"'Well, Skip wanted to fire my ass. Or so says the GM. But

I'm too valuable for them to do that. The White Sox are going to call me up inside of a month—you can bet your balls on it. So it was Old Springs himself came down to minister to me.'

"'Springs' was what we called Osterman, the general manager. He was one of those dynamic guys who walked like he had springs in his shoes, a guy who'd read all those inspirational books like How to Screw Your Friends, Rip Off Your Neighbors, and Make a Million by Age Thirty. He was always talking to us ballplayers about long-term investments, five-year plans, and networking.

"'You're a jerk, McMartin,' he said. Not even a hello. 'You're a screw-up.' He called me ten more names. 'You're also a criminal. If it wasn't for baseball your ass would be in a jail out in the Oklahoma desert, or in a psych hospital, which is where I think you belong. The front-office personnel voted unanimously not to send you flowers or wish you a speedy recovery, Skip said, so he sent me. For some reason, he figures I have more self-control. Skip says to tell you he wishes you'd cut your trouble-making throat when you fell through that window.'

"'Yeah, well you tell Skip his wife's not bad in bed. But she's not nearly as good as your wife.'

"I was sorry as soon as the words were out. I didn't really want those guys to hate me. I just wanted to make it clear that I didn't take crap from anybody.

"'You really are pure filth, McMartin,' Springs growled. 'Unfortunately, in Chicago they think you might hit thirty home runs for them next year. They'd let Charles Manson bat clean-up if they thought he'd hit thirty dingers. But just let me remind you, the minimum wage in Oklahoma is about three-fifty an hour, and out of a uniform you're not even worth that.'

"'Try to imagine how little I care,' I said.

149

"'We're going to tell the press you were being chased out of the building by an angry husband,' said Springs. 'It will fit your image. But let me tell you, even Chicago is fed up with your antics. This is absolutely the last time.'

"'Did management suspend you, or what?' asked Pascoe.

"'Nah, I told you, I'm their fair-haired boy. I'm on the DL. I'll be out of here tomorrow morning. So while you guys head to Portland and Phoenix and get your asses whipped eight out of nine without your clean-up hitter, I'll be sitting in Champagne Charlie's pounding a Bud and drooling over the strippers.'

"'I should have such luck,' said Pascoe. 'I don't know, Barry, you've got to stop acting so . . . so external, man.' He shook his head sadly.

"I should treat Pascoe better, I was thinking. He was a decent guy. I couldn't figure out why he hung with me. When I first arrived he showed me around Vancouver, which bars and clubs to visit, which to stay away from.

"'Stay away from the King's Castle.' he said to me as we walked down Granville Street one evening, heading toward Champagne Charlie's. 'It's the biggest gay bar north of San Francisco. Stay away from the Crown Jewels Bar, too. Lesbians and bikers. Over half the people in that bar have shivs in their boots.'

"There was a flamingo-colored neon sign above the entrance to the King's Castle, and a dozen young men were standing in groups or lounging against the walls near the entrance, all caught in the pinkish glow of the neon.

"'Queers,' I snarled as we passed, not caring if I was heard.

"'Behave yourself,' snapped Pascoe.

"I have to admit I am naturally a loud person. I tend to shout; I walk with a swagger; I keep my head up and my eyes open. I've never minded being stared at; I like it that girls often turn and stare after me on the street.

"Two weeks into the season we were at home against Phoenix. I tripled to lead off the second inning. Pascoe was batting fifth and he popped up weakly to the shortstop. The manager put on the suicide squeeze.

"The pitcher checked me, stretched, and delivered. I broke. The batter bunted, but way too hard. It was whap! snap! and the ball was in the pitcher's glove. He fired to the catcher, a skinny little weasel, who was blocking the plate. I was dead by fifteen feet, but I'd gotten up a real head of steam. I weigh 217, I'm six foot four, and I'd played a lot of high-school football in Oklahoma.

"I hit the guy with a cross block that would have gotten me a starting job in the NFL. I knocked him about five feet in the air, and he landed like he'd been shot in flight. The son of a bitch held onto the ball, though. The guy who bunted was at second before someone remembered to call time. They pried the ball out of the catcher's fingers, and loaded him on a stretcher.

"I'd knocked him toward our dugout and had to almost step over him to get back to the bench. What I saw scared me. His neck was twisted at a weird angle and he was bleeding from the mouth.

"The umpire threw me out of the game for unsportsmanlike conduct. The league president viewed the films and suspended me for five games. The catcher had a concussion, a dislocated shoulder, and three cracked ribs. He was on the DL for sixty days.

"The next time we played Phoenix, I got hit by a pitch my

first time up. Reprisal pure and simple. I charged the mound, and the benches cleared. But before I got to the pitcher, Pascoe, who was in the on-deck circle and must have anticipated me being hit, landed on my back and took me right out of the play Suddenly, there were three or four guys on top of us.

"'Behave yourself,' Pascoe hissed into my ear, as he pinioned me to the ground. Those became Pascoe's favorite words as the summer deepened and I kept finding new ways to get myself into trouble.

"Pascoe was happy when I started going out with Judy. Judy was a friend of a girl he dated, a tiny brunette, a year younger than me, with dancing brown eyes, a student studying sociology. Word even got back to Skip, and he said a couple of civil words to me for the first time since I had cold-cocked the Phoenix catcher.

"'You're just shy,' Judy said to me on our second date.

"'Ha!' cried Pascoe. He and his girlfriend were sitting across from us in a Denny's.

"'It's true,' said Judy. 'People who talk and laugh loudly in order to have attention directed toward them are really very shy.'

"'You are, aren't you? Shy, I mean,' Judy said later that evening in bed at her apartment. Our lovemaking had been nothing spectacular.

"'I suppose,' I said. 'But I'd never admit it.'

"'You just did,' said Judy, leaning over to kiss me.

"Pascoe, Martinez, and I made the rounds of the bars after a Saturday night game. I'd had several beers, but not enough that I should have been out of control. We closed up Champagne Charlie's and decided to walk home. We were approaching

Broadway and Granville, swinging along arm in arm, when a police cruiser pulled up alongside us.

"The passenger window rolled down and an officer, no older than us, said, 'Excuse me, gentlemen, but I'd like to see some identification.'

"Pascoe was reaching for his wallet when I said, 'What are you hassling us for? We're minding our own business.'

"The officer ignored me, but he opened the door and stepped out, accepting the piece of ID Pascoe handed him.

"Martinez, hailing from a country where police do not always exhibit self-control, stayed behind us, looking worried.

"The officer returned Pascoe's ID.

"'And you, sir?' he said to Martinez.

"'Leave him alone,' I said. 'He doesn't speak English.'

"'I'm not addressing you,' the officer said.

"'Leave him alone.' I stepped in front of Martinez.

"'Behave yourself,' said Pascoe, and grabbed my arm. I pushed him away, and before he could recover his balance, I shoved the officer against the car. As the driver was getting out I leapt on the hood.

"What happened next is a blur. I remember screaming curses at the police, dancing madly on the hood of the police car, feeling it dimple under my weight, dodging the grasping hands of the police and Pascoe.

"I remember hearing Pascoe crying out, 'Oh, man, he's just crazy, don't shoot him.' Then there was a hand like a vice twisting on my ankle and I toppled sideways to the pavement. My mouth was full of blood and someone was sitting on me, while my arms were being cuffed behind my back.

"I missed the Sunday afternoon game—management let me

sit in jail until my court appearance Monday morning. The police had charged Martinez with creating a disturbance, but after a translator explained what had happened, the charge was dropped. I faced a half-dozen charges, beginning with assaulting a police officer.

"The judge looked down at me: unshaven, my shirt torn and bloodstained, the left side of my face scraped raw from where I had landed on the pavement. He remanded me fourteen days for psychiatric evaluation.

"'I'm not really crazy,' I said to no one in particular.

"The team lawyer got on the phone to Chicago, and then the White Sox's lawyers got in on the act. Before the end of the day, they struck a deal. If I agreed to spend an hour every afternoon with a psychiatrist, the team would guarantee my good behavior, and my sentencing would be put off until the end of the season. If I kept my nose clean, the sentence would be suspended.

"Management had me by the balls. 'You screw up again and you're gone, kid,' Skip said. 'It doesn't matter how talented you are. I don't care if you're Babe Ruth reincarnated, you're not worth the aggravation.'

"I saw the shrink every afternoon for the whole home stand. I took all these weird tests—questions like 'Are you a messenger of God?' and 'Has your pet died recently?' I wore a jacket and tie to every session and talked a lot about what a nice girlfriend I had and how much I respected my parents.

"'Well, Barry,' the doctor said to me after about ten sessions, 'on the surface you don't appear to have any serious problems, but I do wish you'd make an effort to be more cooperative with me. I'm here to help you with your problems, after all.'

"'I thought I was being cooperative,' I said innocently.

"'You have been, but only partially. I find that you are mildly depressive, that you're anxious, under a lot of stress. Stress is natural in your profession, but there is something else bothering you, and I wish you'd level with me.'

"'Look, I'm okay, honest. I had too much to drink, I got out of control. It won't happen again.'

"'Suit yourself,' said the doctor.

"My life leveled out for almost a month. We went on a road trip. I continued to hit well; I watched the American League standings, studied Chicago's box score in each day's newspaper, watched them fade out of the pennant race. I wondered how much longer it would be before I got my call.

"Once, in Tacoma, Pascoe had to keep me from punching the lights out of a taxi driver who said something insulting about ballplayers, but otherwise I stayed cool. I phoned Judy almost every night. I'd analyze the game, dissect my at-bats pitch by pitch. I doubted that what I was saying was very interesting to her, but it was a release for me, and she seemed to enjoy it.

"Judy brought two friends to a Sunday afternoon home game, on a perfect blue day. The stands at Nat Bailey Stadium are close enough to the field that I could smile over at Judy from the on-deck circle.

"Her friends were a couple, Christine, a bouncy blonde with ringlets and a sexy way of licking her lips, and her husband Trevor, a wimpy guy who wore a jacket and tie to the ballpark and looked like he was shorter than Christine.

"Although I had three hits and two RBIs, I wasn't in a good mood after the game. We went to one of those California-style restaurants with white walls, and pink tablecloths, where everything was served in a sauce, and they looked at you like you just spit on the floor if you asked for french fries. To top it off, I didn't like Trevor, and he didn't like me. I pounded about three Buds and then I drank a whole pitcher of some wine-cooler slop that tasted like Kool-Aid.

"What really threw the crap into the fan was when the three of them decided the four of us would go to a movie, *Kiss of the Spider Woman*, about a couple of queers locked up in a prison in Argentina or someplace. To top it off, Trevor gave us all a little lecture about the eloquent statement the director was trying to make.

"'There's no damn way I'm going to a movie like that,' I said, standing up to make my point.

"'Barry, don't make a scene,' Judy said.

"'No need to be boisterous,' said Trevor. 'You've simply been outvoted. We'd be happy to let you choose, but I don't think *The Texas Chainsaw Massacre* is showing at the moment.'

"I didn't say anything, just grabbed the tablecloth and pushed everything into Trevor's lap, including plates and full water glasses, then turned and stomped out.

"I was surprised when Judy caught up with me a block down the street.

"'You were only half to blame for that one,' she said. 'I'm always willing to go halfway,' she added, taking my arm.

"'I'd rather you went all the way,' I said.

"But things didn't go well back at her apartment.

"'For goodness' sakes, Barry, relax,' Judy said. 'Nobody can make love when they're angry.'

"By that time I was thrashing around the room, pulling my clothes on. Judy continued to talk soothingly to me, but I dashed out of the apartment. Ignoring the elevator, I ran down the stairs, realizing about halfway that I'd forgotten my shoes.

"I crossed the lobby running full out, as if I was on one prolonged suicide squeeze, the catcher twenty feet tall, made of bricks, waiting with the ball, grinning. I didn't even slow down as I hit the wall of glass next to the front door.

"Once I was off the DL and back in the line-up, I picked up right where I had left off—hit two dingers, a single, and stole a base. After each home run, I toured the bases slowly, my head erect, trying to look as arrogant as possible. I had a lot to prove to Skip, to management, and to the self-righteous bastards I played with.

"After the game a note had been shoved through one of the vent slats in my locker. It was written on a paper towel from the washroom, large printing in a childish scrawl.

"'Management pays Pascoe $300 a month to be your friend,' it said. My stomach dipped, and I thought I might vomit. I quickly crumpled the note and stuffed it in my back pocket. I glanced around to see if I could catch anybody watching me. No luck. I'd never ask Pascoe. What if it was true?

"I hate to admit it, but that note got to me. I thought about it more than I ever should have.

"'Let's the three of us stop by Champagne Charlie's,' I said to Pascoe and Martinez as if nothing had happened. 'We can pound a few Buds and eyeball the strippers. There's a new one since you guys have been out of town,' I lied.

"'I thought you had this red-hot date,' said Pascoe.

"'Let her wait.'

"We headed off, three abreast, just like old times. Me in the center, Pascoe to my left, Martinez linked to my right arm.

"'Just like an airplane,' I said, walking fast, watching pedestrians part, or move aside to let us pass.

"'Punchline!' I shouted as we loped along. 'So I stood up, tried to kick my ass, missed, fell off the roof, and broke my leg.'

"Pascoe laughed. Martinez grinned foolishly.

"'The nun had a straight razor in her bra,' said Pascoe, the bluish street lights reflecting off his teeth.

"We swaggered into Champagne Charlie's, got seats at the counter right in front of the stage, ordered a round, and settled in.

"'Man, Canadian beer tastes like gopher piss,' I said, drawing a few ugly stares from the customers. But we knocked back, three each, anyway.

"The stripper was named La Velvet and was very tall and black. She took a liking to Pascoe, winked, and crinkled her nose at him. When she was naked except for red high-heeled shoes, she edged toward us, then, flat on the floor she braced her heels on the edge of the stage, and spread her legs until her crotch was about a foot from Pascoe's face.

"'Way to go, baby,' I yelled.

"Martinez grinned amiably.

"I stood up and clapped in rhythm to her gyrating body.

"'Behave yourself,' hissed Pascoe.

"'Wrap those long legs around his neck!'

"The bouncer came over and tapped me on the shoulder. 'Sit down,' he said.

"I was holding a bottle of beer in my right hand. For half a second I considered smashing it across his face. He was obviously an ex-fighter, with a nose several times broken and heavy scar tissue across his eyebrows. Then I felt Pascoe's hand on my arm.

"'Sit down, Barry,' he growled. 'Why do you always have to act like a troublemaker, man? Why do you have to be bigger and tougher and raunchier and more rough-and-ready than everybody else?'

"I sat down. La Velvet was gathering up her robe and heading down some stairs at the back of the stage.

"'Sorry, I just got carried away,' I said lamely. Pascoe glared at me.

"'Why don't you guys walk over to the restaurant with me?' I asked.

"'Naw.'

"'You want to come for a walk, Marty?'

"Martinez stared at me, smiling, uncomprehending.

"'Walk. Hike. El tromp-tromp. How the hell do you say *walk* in Spanish?'

"Martinez continued to look confused. He glanced from me to Pascoe, as if seeking advice.

"'Walk with me!' I howled, standing up, my beer bottle clutched in my hand. Out of the corner of my eye I could see the bouncer start in our direction.

"'Behave yourself,' said Pascoe urgently. 'We'll come with you, just stop acting like a jerk.' To the bouncer he said, 'We're just leaving. Two drinks and my buddy here thinks he's Tarzan.'

"People were staring at us as we made our way across the night club and up the stairs to the street.

"The movies had just let out, and Granville Street was teeming as we walked along three abreast, arms linked. I forged ahead, the point of the wedge, the pilot. Pascoe relived last evening's game.

"'Man, if I'd just laid back and waited for the slider,' he was saying.

"'Punchline!' I shouted. 'If you can get up and go to work, the least I can do is pack you a lunch.'

"As we rolled along, we passed the shadowy entrance to the King's Castle. One door was open but it was too dark to see inside. A fan expelled the odors of warm beer and cigarette smoke onto the sidewalk. There were several men in the entrance way. Two stood near the doorway, touching, talking earnestly into each other's faces. A tawny-skinned young man in tight Levis, his open white shirt tied in a knot across his belly, leaned insolently against a wall.

"'Queers,' I yelled, pushing on faster.

"'Behave yourself,' snapped Pascoe.

"Beyond the King's Castle I breathed easier. As we were passing, my eyes had flashed across those of the tawny-skinned boy, and I knew that he knew; that it is not a matter of will I or won't I, but only of how long before I do.

"'Punchline!' I wailed. 'Trouble was the pilot was gay.'

"'Ha, ha,' cried Martinez, thinking he understood."

"That's quite a story," I said, not really knowing what to say to a guy who had just bared his soul to me.

"I hope I haven't embarrassed you too much. I've never spoken this stuff aloud."

"It's okay."

We were on the far edge of town. We turned and started back toward the center of Grand Mound.

"So did you?" I asked. "Did you go back to that . . . bar?"

"I would have, but I got in another row. It wasn't my fault. I slid into second on a force play. The second-base man leapt in the air to make the throw to first and came down right on my face. I got my hands around his neck and I was swinging him around like he was a scarecrow stuffed with straw. It took about five people to pull me off him.

"Thirteen more stitches, and I was on the next plane back to Oklahoma.

"They tried all winter to trade me, but there wasn't a team would give me a look. I was all set to go to Japan. I had a try-out with the Nippon Ham Fighters, what a name for a baseball team! I pounded their best pitchers for home runs and line drives for two days. But they must have spies over here, and I guess they were wondering why the White Sox would part with my contract for a song. Anyway, they called me into the office, and there were all these Japanese guys in blue suits sitting around looking sad.

"'You are very talented,' the translator said to me, 'but you have not shown the proper respect for the game of baseball or for your teammates, or for the owners and managers of your teams. Respect is all-important in Japan. Unfortunately, we feel you would have great difficulty fitting in here.'

"It looked like I was out of the game until my agent got a call from someone in Grand Mound. I figured if I kept my nose clean out here in the boonies, sooner or later I'd be forgiven and given another chance. But I behave just as crazy here as anywhere else."

"Maybe, but I think you were on the right track, coming to see me, because you thought I was a studying psychology. Go see a real psychologist or psychiatrist. Tell Suicide Walston—or if you want I'll tell Emmett, so he can tell Walston. If they know you want help, they'll bend over backwards to see you get it. They'll probably pay for it, too."

"The Millers never let on until after I freaked out, but they knew all about my troubles. They seemed to think things would be different in Grand Mound. They still do, even though I'm more or less under house arrest."

"What do you think they're going to do with you?"

"I have no idea."

"Do you think it would help—you know, make you less aggressive, less crazy—if you came out of the closet?"

"In Grand Mound? You're joking! I should have got my nerve up while I was still in Vancouver. I don't know what to do, Mike, that's why I'm taking up your time."

He thanked me for listening, and I promised we'd get together again. But a few days later my own world came crashing down, and I didn't have time to worry about Barry McMartin's problems.

Safe at Home

NINETEEN

What is going on here? I thought that Tracy Ellen and I had this stuff all straightened out. Brother and sister, we agreed. Yet tonight after the game . . .

First, the game: we won 3-2 in eleven innings. In the bottom of the eleventh the bases were loaded with one out. The infield was in so close I could see the color of the batter's eyes. Whack! Stanley Wood hit the ball square on. One hop into my glove. It took me an instant to realize what had happened. Pure luck, nothing to do with my defensive skills, but I can imagine tomorrow's headline in the Grand Mound Leader:

GUNBOAT HOULE DOES IT AGAIN

With the steady nerves of a burglar, Mike "Gunboat" Houle stared down the batter, Stanley Wood, and with the reflexes of a striking snake saved the game for the Whiteshirts. After calmly fielding the blazing grounder, Mike tossed a ribbon of steel to the catcher for the force, and he fired the ball to first for the double play to end the game.

Emmett congratulated me a dozen times as I emerged into

the parking lot from the clubhouse, and we all piled into the Buick, Tracy Ellen and I in the back as usual, Emmett and Marge in the front.

"That was a great play," Tracy Ellen said, as we settled in. She placed her right hand on my left for about two seconds, but the thrill of her touch was like I'd been jabbed with a cattle prod.

"Thanks," I mumbled, and tried to explain how lucky I'd been, but I knew I sounded like I was trying to be modest.

We'd only gone about two blocks when Emmett eased the car to the side of the road.

"Sorry, kids," he said, turning our way, "but I forgot I have to make a stop at the south edge of town; have to pick up some papers from one of the Kittlemeyers. Red and Daisy are sure to invite us in for coffee, and I don't imagine you kids want to be bothered with that sort of stuff. If it's okay I'll just drop you here. Lovely night for a walk."

I looked at Tracy Ellen and shrugged. We got out, and even as Marge was reminding Tracy Ellen about the new carton of ice cream stashed in the freezer, the car swished away, leaving us in the thick, perfumed night air, a ten-foot-tall lilac hedge towering over us. We were only about seven blocks from home, a three-minute drive at most. Why was Emmett in such a rush? I'd been in the office as long as Emmett and I didn't recall any business with the Kittlemeyers.

I glanced at Tracy Ellen, and she smiled at me. Fireflies glimmered like buttons, a sickle of peachy moon hung in the blue-black sky. We walked very slowly. The streets were totally silent. Somewhere far away a dog yapped half-heartedly. My inclination was to sweep Tracy Ellen into my arms. I loved the way her pale hair brushed the shoulders of her blouse.

Our fingertips almost touched. Her lips were parted. Waiting to be kissed? What if I'm wrong? I have to live in the same house as Tracy Ellen, see her several times a day. What if I'm misinterpreting her intentions? It would be so awkward to have her angry with me. Emmett and Marge would wonder what I'd done to make her unhappy. Perhaps she'd even tell them. And she does have a boyfriend.

We continue to walk.

A block from home, in the shadow of a honeysuckle bush, a few tines of distant streetlight flashing through the blossoms, Tracy Ellen stops and turns toward me. I am about to take her in my arms when I see she is pointing down. The white laces of her pink shoe are undone.

"Let me," I whisper. Tracy Ellen places her tiny foot on one of the whitewashed rocks in front of the honeysuckle hedge while I kneel and tie the laces. I turn the cuff of her jeans up an inch or so to make my task easier. She is wearing a delicate perfume that has lime in it. When I stand up, I'll place my hands on her hips, and I'll be able to tell whether she's longing to be kissed.

Just as I finish, the street lights up; it is like the floodlights have been turned on at the ballpark. With the growl of a mastiff, Shag Wilson's truck rumbles toward us. I glance up at Tracy Ellen. Is that a flash of disappointment on her face? I'll probably never know. A moment later, she's gone, and I'm standing on the silent street with only darkness for company.

TWENTY

Just when I think I'm getting some kind of handle on Grand Mound and Tracy Ellen, something new happens that leaves me stunned and puzzled. On my team, the White team, the left fielder is Felix Rincon. Everyone seems to like him a great deal, both as a power hitter and as a person. He's from Vera Cruz, I'm told. Emmett says he was brought in last August as a replacement for an injured player. He spoke passable English, was boarded with Hurchubise the plumber and, though always polite, took no interest in the eighteen-year-old daughter of the house, Nan, who works at the Springtime Café, and now has a definite interest in Stanley Wood. He hit three home runs on the last day of the season, Emmett told me, which assured him of being invited back. He was the first to arrive this spring, and though he's settled in comfortably, Dilly Eastwick still hasn't found a suitable nickname for him.

During Friday night's game, even though it was a 1-1 tie in the seventh, and Felix was due up third in the inning, Suicide Walston waved him out of the game at 9:00 P.M. He disappeared into the clubhouse, and Suicide told the rest of us, "The Hurchubise family have a wedding to attend in Iowa City early tomorrow morning, and they want to take Felix with them to meet other members of the family."

Wow! Get excused from a game to go to a wedding? I wouldn't have thought of making a request like that in high school. But, apparently it wasn't Felix's doing, it was his adopted family's. Still . . .

After the game, which I helped win 2-1 with a tenth-inning walk and stolen base, we returned to the clubhouse to find several members of the Grand Mound Booster Club waiting for us. Dilly Eastwick lavished praise on everyone for such an exciting ball game, singling out me and Dan Morgenstern for special accolades, and finally he got to the point. 'We have a special project going on in town . . ."

"Yeah, the dance," said somebody.

"The dance happens after the game tomorrow night," said Dilly, "and, incidentally, you're all invited. But, no, there's another project—we're restoring a house over on Second Avenue, and since there's no practice tomorrow afternoon we hoped that you all might drop by and give us a hand with the painting and repairs."

"What's the deal?" someone asked suspiciously.

"You'll find out all the details at the dance tomorrow night. In the meantime, trust us, we know what we're doing. The whole project has a lot to do with the Greenshirts, and we know you guys will donate a few hours to help us out."

Dilly's speech and the presence of five other members of the Grand Mound Booster Club, including Emmett, made the request almost an order. I think only Barry McMartin and one other player said they wouldn't be there.

Back at the house, Emmett elaborated a little. "Well, Mike, I don't suppose there's any harm in you getting a bit of a preview. You remember Felix Rincon being called out of the game tonight? Well there was a little more to that than meets the eye. Oh, Hurchubise the plumber and his family do have a wedding in Iowa City, but there wasn't any need to leave early—or even for Felix to go with them. We just wanted to get him out of town until the dance tomorrow night."

Tracy Ellen and Marge had been talking about the dance for several days. It was taking place in the Grand Mound High School auditorium, there was to be a live band, and Tracy Ellen and several of her friends were in charge of decorations. They were using blue spotlights and gels to give the effect of moonlight and stardust.

"Felix is a fine young man, and an outstanding outfielder.

He's a couple of years older than you, but I'd guess he has ten years of solid play in him and we want to keep him here in Grand Mound.

"Now, here's the catch. This spring, he finally admitted that he has a wife and family in Vera Cruz. There's not a thing wrong with that, it just came as a surprise to us. Anyway, first thing we suggested was that he bring his family to Grand Mound.

"'A poor baseball player like myself cannot get a visa for his family to travel with him,' Felix said. 'Besides, it would be very hard for me to support them here. Things are much more expensive than in Mexico.'

"'Just let me investigate that visa business,' said Dilly Eastwick, who, as you've probably learned, is not someone who takes no for an answer.

"Now, this is where tomorrow's project comes in. There's a small house on Second Avenue that's been vacant for years, sort of falling to rack and ruin, as they say. We got hold of the landlord, a widow who lives in a retirement home in Mount Vernon, and she agreed that if we did all the repairs she'd waive the rent for three years, and then maybe sell the house to the Grand Mound Booster Club.

"Felix had apprenticed as a plumber in Mexico, that's why he was boarded at the Hurchubises', so Hurchubise put him to work mornings restoring the plumbing, virtually every pipe in the place needed replacing. The job was finished yesterday, and tomorrow, why, the whole community is going in to paper and paint and decorate, and generally spruce up the house and yard."

"And this has something to do with Felix and his family?"

"You're a quick study, my young friend. Dilly Eastwick has political connections."

"Why doesn't that surprise me?"

"First he phoned Senator Tom Harkin—got him right out of the Senate Chamber—and put the wheels in motion. Then he phoned Senator Charles Grassley and did the same thing. Now, Harkin is a Democrat, and Grassley is a Republican, and I'm sure each one thinks Dilly Eastwick is a life-long supporter, though goodness knows what his political affiliation, if any, may be.

"'It was just like magic,' Dilly said, the way those visas for Felix Rincon's wife and babies arrived at the office of the *Grand Mound Leader*. As for the rest, Mike, you'll just have to wait."

"I'm not sure I understand."

"You will, Mike, you will," said Emmett, leaning toward the fridge and the strawberry pie cooling there.

Next morning when Emmett and I arrived at the house on Second Avenue, there were already a dozen Boosters and players milling around. *Dilapidated* would be the kindest word to describe the place. It had once been a nice cottage, but the years and weather and lack of occupancy had taken their toll. The siding had only a memory of paint, the roof badly needed repair, the lawn was totally overgrown, and a lilac hedge had grown high and wild. The inside was in even worse shape: wallpaper peeling, cupboards sagging, evidence of rodents and weather everywhere.

"Everything is more or less organized," said Dilly Eastwick, who was wearing a pair of baggy railroad coveralls, the sunlight glinting off his thick glasses. "We need to rip off the wallpaper and begin painting. Mike, you paint the east wall of the back bedroom," and he magically produced a half-gallon of peach-colored paint, a roller, and a brush. "When that's done, come see me and I'll have another assignment for you." He took a clipboard from under his arm and made a couple of check marks.

It's amazing what can be done to a small property by forty well-organized people. As the walls were painted, new light fixtures and wall switches were installed. The floors were either tiled or carpeted. New cupboard doors made the kitchen seem larger and certainly brighter. My second assignment was to paint a section of the front of the house, and while I splashed on white paint, Crease Fowler followed with scarlet paint to do the trim around the picture window.

Then, while one crew pruned the hedge, another group cut the lawn, and several people whitewashed bowling-ball-sized rocks, which had appeared on a flat-bed truck, and placed them across the front of the house about three feet out from the foundation, while others transplanted flowers from boxes provided by Grand Mound Nursery. Next, appliances and furniture began arriving: a fridge, an electric stove, a microwave, a washer and dryer for the back porch.

"Nothing new or fancy," Emmett said, as a deep freeze was being maneuvered in the back door. "The Booster Club members are, for the most part, a pretty prosperous lot. We're able to afford to trade things in a little earlier than some folks. Until about an hour ago that deep freeze was in *our* back porch. It's only about five years old, but there's a bigger, newer one being set up at our house right now."

So it went the whole afternoon. When everything was finished, Dilly Eastwick lined everyone up at the front sidewalk, and we walked single file through the front door and out the back admiring our handiwork. Then Dilly added the final touch, a mailbox at the curb that advertised the *Grand Mound Leader* on both sides, but had the name Rincon stencilled on the front.

The dance.

"The one thing we don't have in Grand Mound," Emmett confided, "is a band for all occasions. Now, a few young fellows have garage bands, make a whole neighborhood wear ear plugs, but they usually disband, no pun intended, without ever having played a gig. And there are a couple of country groups with satin shirts and songs about fellows who have lost their girl and their dog's died and their pickup has broken down.

"There's just no satisfying a multi-generational crowd when it comes to music. We've hired the Mount Vernon Legionnaires; they're all past middle age, and they play waltzes and two-steps, and if we asked for it, why, they'd oblige with a square dance (the fiddler doubles as caller), a Virginia reel, a polka, or a schottische. I know the young people will be disappointed, but look at it this way, Mike, there's just no easier way to get close to a girl you like than waltzing to the strains of a sweet old song." And he winked at me.

Emmett Powell winked at me. What a strange town this is.

I have to agree with Emmett's assessment of waltzing. There were couples on the dance floor where it was impossible to see where one person left off and the other began. I danced with Nan Hurchubise, when Stanley Wood's back was turned. Then I approached Tracy Ellen as the band began "The Tennessee Waltz."

"Is Shag gonna mind if I borrow you for one dance?" I asked.

Tracy Ellen took my hand and led me to the floor, placing her free hand gently on the back of my neck, and laying her head on my shoulder.

171

"Shag doesn't dance," she said. "He'll pick me up later."

"You did a wonderful job with the decorations," I said. The Grand Mound High School had been transformed into a moon-lit glade surrounded by fluttery-leafed aspens. The Mount Vernon Legionnaires were dressed in blue blazers and grey flannels.

"Do you like it?" Tracy Ellen smiled up at me, then pressed herself closer. I was glad Shag Wilson was out doing whatever thugs like him did while they waited for their girlfriends to finish dancing.

Glancing over Tracy Ellen's shoulder I was surprised by how many ballplayers had local girls as partners, Stanley with Nan Hurchubise, Dan Morgenstern and Becky, myself and Tracy Ellen.

I danced another half-dozen dances with Tracy Ellen. The message from her body was positive.

About 10:30 P.M. there was a food break. Buffet tables were so loaded, it looked just like Marge Powell's kitchen. I spotted Felix Rincon sitting with the Hurchubise family at a table near the front. Emmett took to the stage, blowing and tapping on the microphone, like people not used to speaking in public do.

"Anybody know how the rat lost his tail? Catnip. Hah! Did you folks hear about the newlyweds who were given a house by their combined families? Sort of left them home free." Complete silence was followed by a chorus of happy groans.

"You know," Emmett went on, "when we have an event like this there's usually some sort of surprise involved. Well, I'd like to call our star outfielder Felix Rincon up here because we have a surprise for him—more than one actually."

The Hurchubise family pushed Felix toward the stage; in fact, Nan accompanied him to the bottom of the stairs. He walked shyly to the center of the stage and shook hands with Emmett. He was obviously puzzled.

But Emmett prolonged the suspense by introducing Dilly Eastwick. Dilly handled the microphone like a pro. "Ladies and gentlemen," he began, "you all know what an outstanding job Felix has been doing for us in the outfield. Who'll ever forget those three home runs on the final day of last season?" There was a smattering of applause. "Well, we've discovered something about Felix that most of you don't know." He paused for dramatic effect. "Felix is a papa, three times over." More applause.

I've always wondered about someone receiving applause for the simple act of reproduction, like at a retirement: "Good old Gus has five children and twenty-eight grandchildren." Reams of applause—as if Gus had invented penicillin.

"Felix has a lovely wife, Maria Esmerelda, a son, Felix Jr., a daughter, Carmelita, and another son, Juan. Now we at the Grand Mound Booster Club know that none of us would like to be away from our families from April to September, so we got together and . . ." Dilly gestured toward a curtain to his right, which was swept aside, and there was a dark stocky woman, two tiny children beside her, another clutched to her chest, and obviously eight months or more pregnant. She had black braids tied with red wool, and a wide, warm face.

"Papa! Papa! Papa!" the older children screamed when they saw their father, and half ran, half danced their way across the stage. The wife moved more slowly and was met by Felix, a child securely anchored to each leg. I doubt that there was a dry eye in the house as Felix and Maria Esmerelda hugged, and he kissed her and then the baby nodded sleepily on her shoulder. Tracy Ellen held tightly to my hand, a tear oozing down her cheek.

The whole auditorium stood and applauded for the Rincons, for the Grand Mound Booster Club, and for ourselves. No group of people anywhere in America could have felt better about themselves and their neighbors at that moment.

Since there is no car rental in Grand Mound, the Booster Club had improvised—one of the grey luxury cars from Beckman Funeral Parlor was waiting outside for the Rincons. Maria Esmerelda is crying as she is helped into the cavernous back seat. Felix holds a child in each arm, they are kissing him and murmuring, "Papa! Papa!"

The car glides away from the curb, but the town is not yet satisfied. A procession forms and moves away from the school, ragged, unsure, like a picture one sees in history books of religious pilgrimages. There is a little shriek of siren as Constable Andrews, a large man with sad, hound-dog eyes, every button straining against the cloth of his uniform, eases the Grand Mound police car to the head of the improvised parade. We turn on Jefferson Avenue, then a block later onto Second Avenue, moving along with controlled excitement, people chattering like magpies. As we left the school, Tracy Ellen had excused herself and disappeared. I had been so hopeful. I suppose Shag Wilson is lurking out there somewhere in his souped-up monstrosity.

At the renovated house we stand around on the street and sidewalk just staring happily at the town's handiwork. Mrs. Thoman from the library, and Mrs. Ogilvie, the Spanish teacher from Grand Mound High School, are showing the Rincons around. Every light in the house is on. Occasionally, we can see shadows behind curtains. Emmett and Marge have found me; they are holding hands. Then the front door opens and Mrs. Ogilvie and Mrs. Thoman come out, and the crowd disperses.

"Quite a day's work," says Emmett, sighing.

"It is," I reply.

"Everybody wins. We add four, and soon five, to the population of Grand Mound. Father Damien over at St. Scholastica will be beaming. Aren't you proud to be part of something like this, Mike? There's an old song, a hymn, the words are something like 'I wake each morning, Lord, with fire beneath my skin.' It's meant to be about evangelical fervor, which isn't our way, but it does describe how I feel. Mike, I just can't wait for tomorrow. I've got such a wonderful family, I live in the greatest little town in the world, and there are so many things that still need doing."

"I understand," I say. And I do. I feel very close to Emmett and to Grand Mound, and if Tracy Ellen were here holding my hand, everything would be perfect, and I too, could stay in Grand Mound forever.

In the morning edition of the *Grand Mound Leader*, Dilly Eastwick wrote modestly of the Grand Mound Booster Club arranging to fly in the family of home-run-hitting outfielder, Felix "Papa" Rincon.

TWENTY-ONE

My dad is getting married. After three weeks, three weekends, and a trip together to the Quad Cities, Dad and Peggy McNee are engaged. Gilbert Houle, who's seldom dated, never had a girlfriend stay the night, is getting married to a woman he's known for three weeks.

The thought astounds me.

Are you taking her back to Chicago?" was my first question.

"Of course not," Dad answered, as if my question was stupid. He's lived within thirty miles of downtown Chicago all his life.

"We'll be living here." We were sitting on the end of the

first-base bleacher after a game. The sunset sky was a mottled black and orange, a mammoth monarch butterfly.

"At Peggy's," he went on.

"What about your job?"

"They have a lumberyard here, Son. Emmett was kind enough to check things out for me. I went in for an interview this afternoon. They've got a retirement coming up. I'll pretty well be in charge of the outdoor section of the yard. It will be a step up, though the salary will be lower. But in a small town, living's not so expensive."

"And the house? Our house?"

"Byron wants to stay in the Chicago area after he graduates. He can pay the mortgage just like rent, at first. Then as he becomes established I'll let him buy it. Has he mentioned to you that he's getting married as soon as he graduates?"

"He has. And how do you feel about that?"

"'If his old man's getting married before he is, there isn't a whole lot I can say. Not that I don't like Linda, they're just so young. But then, your mom and I were hardly out of high school."

"You've thought of everything."

"Aren't you happy for me?"

"I don't like to see you rush into something."

"Mike, your mom's been dead for nearly twenty years. You boys have lives of your own. I don't call that rushing."

"Still . . ."

"What's your problem, Mike. Don't you like Peggy?"

"She's fine."

What was my problem? Why was I giving my dad a bad time by holding back my approval of his marriage?

"In spite of what you might think, Mike, young people aren't the only ones who enjoy sexual attraction . . ."

"It's not that, Dad."

The thought suddenly strikes me that I may have been re-cruited to play baseball in Grand Mound simply to lure my father here. Peggy's husband died of leukemia when he was only in his early thirties. Tracy Ellen said there was a huge insurance policy, something Peggy's husband bought through dumb luck when he was first out of high school. The annual payout, which was large to begin with, was adjusted with inflation. Consequently, Peggy's daughter—Brenda? Barbara? Bernice?—went to exclusive prep schools in the East and was accepted by Harvard—or was it Yale?—where she met and married a medical student from Iowa. He now practices in Cedar Rapids, and she's a stockbroker.

Emmett and the Grand Mound Booster Club—perhaps their project this season was to find a husband for Peggy McNee. I could see them in one of their weekly meetings at the Doll House Café, Dilly Eastwick consulting the dog-eared black book that lives like a hamster in the pocket of his shirt, squinting from his beady little eyes, saying, "According to my calculations Peggy McNee has been a widow for thirteen years. Her daughter has set up residence in Cedar Rapids, a loss of one in population for Grand Mound.

"Now, I think it's our duty to find Peggy McNee a husband. I move that we make our spring semester project the acquiring of a suitor for Peggy McNee. Perhaps we could call it the Suitable Suitor Project," and Dilly would laugh his squeaky, irritating laugh, while everyone else remarked on how clever he was.

"I haven't told you the other good news, Mike."

I wonder how much good news I can take.

"There's more?" I ask.

"You know how I've always dreamed of coaching? How as a young man I wanted to go to university and teach and coach?"

"Yeah."

'Well, I'm going to coach for the Greenshirts. Actually, I'll be on your team. The White team. I had a meeting with Dilly Eastwick and all the fellows who administer the club, and they're gonna issue me a white uniform just like yours, Mike.

"I'll be first-base coach for the White team. It's a start. Surely I'm capable of standing in the coach's box and watching the pitcher for a move to first when our runner's leading off. I can shout 'Back!' as loud as the next guy, when the pitcher makes a pick-off throw to first. And if the runner doesn't read the steal sign, I can whisper in his ear, 'Run as soon as he releases the ball you dumb son of a bitch.'"

"It sounds great, Dad. You'll make a terrific coach. I'll try not to get picked off first too often. So when do you start?"

"Walston says I can coach tomorrow. Then full time as soon as I can get moved down here, which shouldn't take more than another week or so. I've already put in my resignation at Schiffert Box and Lumber."

"Sounds great," I said again.

"Look, Son, I realize I've got to make a new life for myself here with Peggy. But I'm also going to be able to keep my promise—if Byron takes over the house, I'll never have to take your mom's photos down."

"Dad, it would be all right if you did." But we both know I haven't given my full approval. And I'm sure neither of us can figure out why.

TWENTY-TWO

"Dan Morgenstern is gone," Dilly Eastwick announces. He and Mrs. Thoman from the library are at the door, and Dr. Greenspan's Mercedes is pulling up at the curb. They are all members of the Grand Mound Booster Club. "If Grand Mound were a country, the Booster Club would be the cabinet," Emmett has told me.

"Gone where?" asks Emmett, looking puzzled.

"Suicide Walston left mid-afternoon to drive him to Cedar Rapids to get the plane back home to New Jersey."

Emmett nods. "Would you excuse us, Mike. This is baseball club business."

"Lew Gainer from the Feed and Seed is on his way over," says Dilly, as Dr. Greenspan joins them and they make their way to Emmett's office.

"He thundered into my office, early this morning, mad as a wet hen," says Dilly Eastwick. "I did my best."

"What's going on?" I ask Marge and Tracy Ellen.

"Why don't I make some coffee and we'll all have cherry pie and ice cream when their meeting is over," says Marge.

Tracy Ellen looks as if she wants to tell me something. She reaches her hand out to me, then thinks better of it.

"I don't know," says Tracy Ellen.

"What do you mean you don't know? What could Dan have found out that sent him back East in a huff? He and Becky seemed to get along so well . . ."

"Shhh!" says Tracy Ellen, nodding toward the living room.

There by the dim light of a pole lamp I see Becky Greenspan and another girl sitting on the sofa. Becky is wearing sunglasses with a kerchief tied over her dark hair, looking like Audrey Hepburn.

"Come on," I say. "I need some information."

"I don't know anything," says Tracy Ellen with some authority, walking past me and into the living room.

I go to my room. I lie down with my ear to the polished hardwood and try to hear what is going on in Emmett's study. Nothing. I listen at the heating vent. I can hear words being spoken, but can make out nothing. What is going on here? I really liked Dan Morgenstern, and he seemed to like it here in Grand Mound. What could have happened in the last twenty-four hours to make him unhappy enough to leave Grand Mound, his adopted family, and Becky?

There is something not right here in Grand Mound. There is something unnatural about the townspeople's fanaticism for baseball. There is something extremely odd about a full house for afternoon practices and standing room only at every evening inter-squad game. There is something not right about the voluntary isolation accepted by most of the baseball players. There is something not right in that after almost five weeks of practices and inter-squad games, no one has been cut from the roster.

There is something not right about Dilly Eastwick and his newspaper; the praise he heaps on us players is comforting, pleasurable, like providing a child unlimited access to ice cream, but it is as if each column is written by a close relative of the player being praised. Errors and bonehead plays, a throw to the wrong base, a missed hit-and-run sign, though they are few in number, are never mentioned in the *Grand Mound Leader.*

There is something not right about our manager, Gene "Suicide" Walston, and his coaches. They have made no attempt to play the best combination of players as a team; in fact, the line-up is often adjusted at the last moment in order to give both teams balance, to make the inter-squad game as even as possible—as if we are going to keep on playing inter-squad games forever.

There is something, not right about families, especially families with marriageable daughters, competing to house the baseball players.

I'm sure there is a tie-in between us ballplayers and the overwhelming enthusiasm for small-town life of Emmett and his friends from the Grand Mound Booster Club. But what is that connection? Is there some common denominator in our being chosen to play baseball here in Grand Mound?

I've been here well over a month, though at times it feels like only moments. At other times it seems I have lived my whole life here. The one thing I know is that I have never been happier.

I'm assured by both Emmett and Coach Walston that the Cornbelt League will begin play in a few days. Walston even took me to a storeroom under the stands and showed me banners that will be hung across Main Street and on the front of Fred Noonan Field, welcoming the Mechanicsville baseball club to opening night in Grand Mound.

The afternoon practices continue, the evening inter-squad games continue. We work at our jobs in the morning. We are playing powerful baseball. I'm sure we'll be the class of the league. Our families wait for us after every game to take us home.

It is as if they are afraid we will discover something if left to our own devices.

* * * * *

About forty-eight hours ago I got a phone call from Justin Birdsong.

"There's an opening at Double A Knoxville," he said. "A rash of injuries, serious ones. You'll be able to play at least until the All-Star break. If you put up big numbers, no telling where you could end up."

I turned him down cold. I didn't even take overnight to think about it.

"I'm playing great baseball here," I said. "As soon as the league starts I'm gonna be tearing up the pea patch. As soon as a couple of scouts see me, I'll probably get bumped right up to Triple A, maybe with a major-league organization that's a contender."

Justin Birdsong argued for me to report to Knoxville.

"I don't know when I've ever been happier," I said. "I want to play in the Cornbelt League for a month or so. I sort of feel I owe them after all they've done for me."

"Suit yourself," said Justin Birdsong, "but don't expect an opportunity like this to come along again soon."

But when I think of playing in Double or Triple A, even when I think of the Cornbelt League opening in a few days, my back tightens and the lump of live anxiety that has followed me all my playing days reappears. I had hoped it had gone away, but it was only lurking in the night.

When I think of the pressure of playing professional baseball, pressure from the fans who expect perfection from professionals, pressure from the manager and the coaches, and most of all from myself . . . the voices of all my past managers and coaches blend together like crows scrapping: close your shoulders, level your swing, even your stance, hit on the ground, take an outside pitch to the opposite field, cover the bag, turn the pivot, on your toes, glove on the ground, back up the base, take the cut-off, and on and on.

With all those snappish voices whirling about my head, I freeze, mind and body blank as snow. The green perfection of the baseball field becomes a bad dream. My stomach feels full of broken glass.

I remember one of my last games at LSU, jolting awake at my position when I should have been covering first base on a sacrifice play. The first-base man charged the ball, the pitcher fielded the bunt cleanly but had no one to throw to because I had been daydreaming and had failed to cover first.

The fans jeered, the pitcher slammed the ball into his glove as he stalked back toward the mound, glowering at me. The manager, his eyes glowing in the dusk of the dugout, spit in my direction. I learned later that there had been at least a half-dozen major-league scouts at that game. No wonder my stock plummeted until I wasn't drafted at all.

The idea of playing professional baseball terrifies me. I want to play here in Grand Mound, where baseball is fun, where my family meets me after each game. Where I feel I belong.

I am a big fish in a very small pond, and I like it. I am doing something I love with all my heart, for the sheer joy of doing it. Can anything be wrong with that?

Yes. And what is wrong can be summed up in two words: Tracy Ellen. I've come to care for Emmett as if he were a favorite uncle, a second father, an over-friendly St. Bernard dog who, in his enthusiasm jumps up, paws on shoulders, nearly causing mayhem. Marge is the mother I've never known. My father has been reeled in by Grand Mound, seduced by it and by Peggy McNee.

In three weeks my father has altered his whole life. I'm happy for him. Why I can't let him know is a mystery to me.

But, what's wrong is Tracy Ellen. If I'm going to stay here, even only for the summer, I've got to set things straight with Tracy Ellen. I've got to let her know how I feel about her, let her know this brother-sister business has to end, that I want to be competition for Shag Wilson. Hell, I want to run Shag Wilson out of the state.

I daydream about Tracy Ellen. Two nights ago, I made an error, a routine ground ball that I let play me, that I didn't get a jump on because I was daydreaming about kissing Tracy Ellen, about enfolding her in my arms. If I could have told her after the ballgame that I made the error because I was daydreaming about her, we could have laughed about it. Tracy Ellen would have said, "I expect I'll have to pay a lot more attention to you off the field so you can keep your mind on the game."

TWENTY-THREE

I did not sleep that whole night. Well, I did doze off, but only long enough to have one of those trapped dreams. I was at second base and an inning-ending double-play ball was hit toward me, but I was unable to move, and the ball went bouncing harmlessly past me while I stood like a statue. The play occurred several times in a row. I could hear the fans booing, my teammates cursing. I tried to explain, but I was paralyzed, as if my cleats were two feet long and driven deep into the earth like the spikes that anchor the bases.

As the dream continued, a bunt was laid down, and once again I was unable to race to first base to take the throw for the pitcher. My worst fear had been realized, I had once again failed to cover first on a sacrifice. I woke, my stomach burning as if I'd swallowed a hot coin.

I think I may actually have had an ulcer my final year at LSU. When things were going so badly for me, the burning pain at the base of my breastbone plagued me when I woke each morning, and every time I became hungry. I chomped antacids, drinking off chalky liquids between innings from a bottle I kept under the bench. But my health has been fine here in Grand Mound. Until now. It's Tracy Ellen, I tell myself; but I know it's also the uncertainty of what is going on with the baseball team.

The meeting in Emmett's study seemed to go on and on all night. I considered slipping downstairs and outside and peering in the window like a burglar in hopes of finding out what happened. Instead, I dozed fitfully until Marge called me for a late breakfast. Emmett, looking tired, was not his jovial self.

One of the things I learned in business school was to face your problems, because they won't go away on their own; take a stand—confront and conquer.

"Why did Dan Morgenstern leave?" I ask between mouthfuls of oatmeal covered with brown sugar and cream. I think I hear a small intake of breath from Marge, who is standing at the kitchen sink. Tracy Ellen has not appeared.

Emmett locks me in a dour stare.

"Things aren't always the way they seem, Mike. Or the way we'd like them to be. Dan is a fine young man; however, he decided that he has better baseball prospects elsewhere than the Cornbelt League. We'd never dream of standing in the way of a young man's ambition."

"Specifically what changed his mind so suddenly?"

"There were a lot of factors involved, Mike, things having to do with internal policies toward players, matters involving individual players and management."

"Bafflegab," I said.

"Pardon?"

"Bafflegab. That's what we called a statement like that in business school. It says a lot, but at the same time says nothing."

"It's the best I can do, son," says Emmett, pulling nervously at his tie.

We stay out of each other's way the remainder of the day.

The locker room is quiet as a tomb before the game. Some societies never speak the names of the dead, and this appears to be one of them. No one mentions Dan Morgenstern. Suicide Walston uses a back-up catcher and says matter-of-factly that a new catcher will be arriving tomorrow from Cleveland.

I'm tempted to ask if he'll be assigned to the Greenspans as a replacement, or if they've dropped to the bottom of the list of townspeople waiting to board a ballplayer.

The house is very quiet after the game. Tracy Ellen is out with Shag Wilson. I go to bed early, and sleep until almost dawn. I wake to my advice from business school. Take a stand. Confront. Conquer.

I dress quickly. To get downstairs, I have to walk right past Tracy Ellen's room, but I don't want to take the chance of frightening her by knocking on, or opening her door; and I particularly don't want to have Emmett catch me in his daughter's bedroom at 5:00 A.M. I slip out the front door, and around the side of the house. I take a small pebble and toss it at Tracy Ellen's window. I hit the siding a good two feet to the right of the window. Some ballplayer I am.

Eventually I get the rhythm, and tiny pellets are plinking

off the glass. A dozen pebbles later, there is no response. Perhaps Tracy Ellen is a heavy sleeper.

I remember when Byron was about ten, one of his friends wanted to call on him very early Sunday morning, my dad's day to sleep late. The friend had been warned never to phone or knock on our door before 10:00 A.M. on Sundays. He decided to toss pebbles at Byron's window, which, unfortunately, was on the same side of the house as Dad's window. Byron, who has always slept like he was in a coma, didn't hear a sound, but Dad did.

Dad, who is normally as good-humored as a man can be, charged out the front door and around the corner of the house, looking like a caveman in boxer shorts. Dad threatened that if he ever saw the poor kid on our property or heard him on our telephone before he turned twenty-one, he would suffer unspecified irreparable damage. By the time Dad had finished, the boy was a couple of blocks away.

Byron's friend didn't stay scared more than a couple of days, and the incident has become one of those tales of a family's mythology. The friend is now a senior at Notre Dame, and when he is home, he and my dad often reminisce about the day Dad threatened his life.

About the twentieth time I bounce a pebble off her window, Tracy Ellen appears at the glass, and I beckon for her to come down. She pushes the window up, leans out.

"What?"

"I need to talk to you. It's important."

"Come up here."

"No. Away from the house."

"Why?"

"Please come down."

"Just a minute."

She disappears. About two minutes later she slips out the front door. Her hair is tangled, her startled eyes still sleep-hazed. She is wearing jeans and a well-worn denim jacket over a pink turtleneck.

"What is it, Mike?"

"I've been awake most of the night. There are things I've got to talk to you about. Let's walk."

I take Tracy Ellen's arm, and we head down the gentle slope of the ridge toward town. The sun is just thinking about coming up, pink tendrils are crawling up the horizon, turning the eastern sky a warm, delicious pink.

"I have to ask you something that may not be any of my business."

"If it's important enough to get me up at five o'clock in the morning, it's important enough to ask."

"How serious are you about Shag Wilson?"

The hill allows us a full view of the sunrise, the magic of dawn is turning the sky an ever-deepening red. Anyone viewing us would see only our black silhouettes against the fiery background of sunrise.

Tracy Ellen stops and turns toward me.

"Not as serious as you might think."

I can feel my heart slamming in my throat. The dew-sweet morning air is fresh as new ironing.

"Meaning?"

"Meaning just that. I like him. He likes me. We're not about to run off and get married. Why is how I feel about him so important?"

"Because I'm tired of this brother-sister agreement. And I

hope you are, too."

I've got to play this cool. I've got to restrain myself. My impulse is to lunge at Tracy Ellen, to fold her into my arms, to kiss her and touch her . . . and probably frighten her away.

"That's really nice, Mike. I'm flattered."

She smiles at me. Against the scarlet sky, the fire of it turning the tips of her pale, tangled hair orange, she looks so vulnerable. I don't think I have ever wanted anyone so much.

"I know it's awkward with us living in the same house, though as much as I hate to admit it, I guess your dad knew what he was about . . . trying to pair us off and all." Don't blow it, Mike. Don't blow it . . . "I'm not trying to make decisions for you, Tracy Ellen, I just want you to know . . ."

"Mike, I understand."

Tracy Ellen takes my hands in hers. The look in her eyes tells me I'm not wasting my time.

I am about to gently pull her into my arms when the whole brilliant morning sky behind her seems to flash me a message. It's not a hallucination, there is nothing written on the sky. It is just that I am suddenly overwhelmed with information, with knowledge I have felt, but not quite known. Knowledge that has been creeping up on me ever since I arrived in Grand Mound, stalking me on clever cat feet.

I remember on what must have been my seventh Christmas, Dad and Byron and I were decorating the tree when the revelation that there was no Santa Claus came upon me. I feel exactly the same way now; convulsed with shattering, world-changing knowledge.

I know what is going on here in Grand Mound. I know what is not right, and why it is not right. I know why Dan Morgenstern left Grand Mound in anger.

How could I not have seen it before?

"What's the matter?" Tracy Ellen says. There are tiny lines, a little V between her brows as she stares at me, puzzled by my almost catatonic state.

Tracy Ellen is gently pulling me toward her. What I have been fantasizing about for days is about to become fact, and I can't let it happen.

I pull my hands back.

"What's wrong?" says Tracy Ellen. "I thought . . ."

"You know all about it, don't you?"

"About what?"

"What you've all been doing to me. Well, it's not going to be that easy."

"Mike!" There is genuine concern on Tracy Ellen's face. "Ask me anything. I can explain . . ."

"No, you can't," I almost shout. "Everything is changed. You've been deceiving me."

Before Tracy Ellen can say anything else I turn and run blindly down the hill, toward the bluish, sleeping town not yet touched by the magic of dawn.

Magic Time

TWENTY-FOUR

I feel like I'm being slapped across the face, banged against walls every way I turn. I am furious. How could they do this to me?

What if I'm wrong? What if the information I've just intuited is totally off base? What if it is a defense mechanism, something to keep me from developing a relationship with Tracy Ellen? What if I don't want what I think I want?

I'll confront Emmett the second he gets to work. I walk aimlessly up and down the green, leaf-sheltered streets of Grand Mound. Daylight has broken, I know it will only be a short time until the Doll House Café opens. I think of the corny jokes Emmett is always telling. "Why did the night owl go home? It dawned on him." I'll get Mrs. Nesbitt to cook me a good breakfast. Then, since I have my own key to the office, I'll lie in wait for Emmett and we'll have things out.

The Doll House opens at 6:00 A.M. I'm making my third circle of the block—the lights are on inside and I imagine I can smell coffee percolating as I wait for the "closed" sign on the front door to be reversed—when I hear the familiar purr of

Emmett's Buick. I duck between two buildings as the car cruises by, Emmett, hair dishevelled, a jacket thrown over pajamas, behind the wheel. Tracy Ellen must have wakened him.

I can't go to breakfast or to the office. I could leap out in the street and confront Emmett now. But something holds me back. What if I'm making a fool of myself? I will stay out of sight until the Grand Mound Library opens at ten. There is something I want to check out. Then I'll take on Emmett and Dilly Eastwick, and whoever else I have to.

I decide the ballpark is the least likely place Emmett will look for me. The gate is chained shut. Roger Cash's key is not where he usually hides it. Try as I might, I can't force myself though the narrow space created by the slackness of the chain. I back off, take a short run and land with one foot on the chain, using it as a thrusting point to catapult myself upward just enough to grab onto the top of the fence with both hands. With some struggle I pull myself over the fence and make the long jump to the ground.

The grass of the field is still covered in dew, the stadium silent as a holy place. I walk slowly from first base to the center-field wall, marvelling at the tracks I leave, a trail of silvered footprints. I am overcome with sadness at the thought that I may have played my last game here.

Looking around this serene little stadium I understand why Roger Cash settled here. But if I'm right, and I'm certain I am, I will never forgive Emmett and the citizens of Grand Mound for the way they've treated me, for what they've concealed from me.

As the morning warms, I stretch out on the top row of the first-base bleacher to catch the morning sunlight full on. I sleep, then wake with a start. I'm sure I hear Emmett's car crunch across the parking lot. The hum of the motor has a distinctive timber. The car stops for a moment by the gate. I hear the car door open, then slam. I hear Emmett's footsteps on the gravel, can picture him studying the gate into Fred Noonan Field. He must decide there is no way I could be inside, for his steps recede. The car door opens and closes, The car pulls away and the sound of it gradually recedes until I am again alone in sunshine and silence.

As ten o'clock approaches, I walk very carefully, by back streets, to the Grand Mound Library, an old, stone-pillared building with a semi-circle of low concrete steps up to the door. One of the original Carnegie endowments, Emmett told me proudly. The minute Mrs. Thoman, the librarian, unlocks the front door I squeeze inside.

"Well, Gunboat, how may I help you?" Mrs. Thoman is a sturdy little woman in a blue crepe dress.

"I'd like to see the *Grand Mound Leader* for the current month, but from, say, three and four years ago."

I find it embarrassing to be addressed by my nickname, especially by this cross-looking, matronly grandmother. But I also know she never misses a game, and somehow, in spite of holding this full-time job, manages to be present at most afternoon practices. I will have to read quickly, for Mrs. T. is a member of the Grand Mound Booster Club.

"Are you certain you want to do that?" Mrs. Thoman asks, in what I'm sure is her best grandmotherly way.

"Why wouldn't I?" I say. "I'm a great fan of Dilly Eastwick. I just want to read some of his past columns."

Actually, for all his good humor and sincerity, for all the

praise and nicknames he heaps on the players, there is something sneaky about Dilly Eastwick, not exactly evil, but furtive. He seems to be looking over his shoulder. After a game, even while he is smiling, praising my play, shaking my hand, his eyes are somewhere in the corner of the room. I expect to see Dilly Eastwick's photo flashed on one of these television crime-solving shows. I surmise that in a past life he embezzled a million dollars from his employer, perhaps poisoning a nagging wife, leaving behind dazed friends and relatives who tell the police, "He was a nice guy. Always quiet and polite."

Mrs. Thoman turns away without speaking. The library smells of dry paper and varnished wood.

She returns a few moments later with an armful of newspapers and deposits them on an oak table.

"Here you are, Gunboat," she says, giving me a knowing look. "I'm looking forward to the game tonight. You know, you're the best second-base man we've had in Grand Mound in over twenty years."

"Thank you. That's very kind of you."

"It's true. Just keep it in mind, that's all I ask."

As I turn through the newspapers, Mrs. Thoman makes a number of phone calls. Though I try, I cannot make out any of her whispered conversation.

I only have to read through a half-dozen newspapers to confirm my suspicions. Four years ago, Dilly Eastwick wrote, "Last night, our new second-base man for the Green team, Lew 'Gunboat' Driscoll, danced like Baryshnikov all around the infield, handling six chances flawlessly, while turning the pivot on two double plays and taking a high throw but still managing to cut down a speedy runner attempting to steal."

194

A day later, he wrote, "August Marsh threw a clothesline to second base in the seventh inning to nail a runner. The flight path of the ball was so straight and true that it remained marked in the air for innings." Dilly closed by saying, "August 'Clothesline' Marsh is going to have an outstanding season for the Greenshirts."

There it was, exactly as I suspected. There *was* something sneaky about Dilly Eastwick. Everyone in Grand Mound was sneaky. Lew "Gunboat" Driscoll had my nickname. I hadn't met Lew Driscoll, but I had heard he had retired after suffering a career-ending ankle injury last season. He was still in Grand Mound. He had married a local girl during his first few months here. They have a child, another on the way, a small home. Lew Driscoll drives a truck for the local heating-oil dealer.

I try to imagine a meeting of the Grand Mound Booster Club, maybe even with Lew Driscoll present. There would be some secret ceremony where the name "Gunboat" is retired; a moment when Gunboat Driscoll, second-base man, becomes Lew Driscoll, truck driver and permanent resident of Grand Mound. Possibly he is inducted into the Grand Mound Boosters at the same time his nickname is repossessed.

Until this morning, it appears that I was the only person in Grand Mound, with the possible exception of Stanley Wood, who did not understand what was going on. Now I know why.

When I've pressed team members to make a trip to other towns in the Cornbelt League or to Iowa City or the Quad Cities to catch a baseball game or go looking for girls, they look at me strangely and decline, claiming some obligation to their real or adopted families. There is something odd about an unattached baseball player who does not want to go into the night searching for girls. How many of the baseball players have married local girls? Half? More than half? Is there something evil going on here? I remember a movie called *The Stepford Wives*. Are local girls being raised to be baseball brides?

I suddenly remember a line of Casey Stengel's that Dad used to quote whenever the subject of chasing girls came up, "Being with a woman never hurt a ballplayer, but being out all night looking for woman, that's what does them in."

And last week Emmett announced, just as we were dressing for afternoon practice, that opening day had had to be postponed because several of Mechanicsville's college players had not arrived. Not one of the players batted an eye. It was as though they were expecting the announcement, an announcement that I now see was probably made for my benefit alone.

Everyone in Grand Mound, including Tracy Ellen, is laughing at me.

Well, no more.

I return the newspapers to Mrs. Thoman's desk.

"Did you find what you were looking for, Gunboat?"

"Yes, I did. You know, Dilly Eastwick is really a very fine sports writer. I'll bet he could catch on in the big city if he set his mind to it."

It was my intention to walk over to the office and confront Emmett, but just as I open the front door of the library, the Buick pulls up at the curb. Emmett leaps out and walks around the car toward me. He has changed into his usual grey business suit, his tie hangs loose around his neck.

"Mike, I've been looking everywhere for you. Get in the car. There are some things I have to explain."

Emmett heads the car out of Grand Mound, on a narrow

county road, like a pencil line between fields of new corn.

"I expect you have some questions?" Emmett begins.

"I certainly do, Emmett. First of all, Grand Mound doesn't really have a team in the Cornbelt League, do they? Be honest with me."

The sun is blazing out of a high, clear sky. Heat waves are already rising from the pavement in front of us.

"Well now . . ."

"My agent was given to believe he'd found me a high-class amateur league where the big-league scouts looked in regularly . . ."

"Well, now, Mike, your agent's way out in California, and what he doesn't know about Iowa would fill a book or two. When we were negotiating we may have exaggerated a bit, stretched the truth if you will . . ."

"Like lying about Grand Mound being a member of the league?"

"Mike, we have the league's word that if a team ever drops out, or if a franchise fails, why, Grand Mound gets first opportunity to enter a team."

"For how long?"

"Pardon?"

"How many years has Grand Mound been waiting?"

"Folks here in rural Iowa are set in their ways, Mike. Things don't change much, and when they do, they change slowly."

"HOW LONG?"

"We've . . . we've been in our present holding-pattern situation since just after World War II."

I am so frustrated by this deception that I can hear tears in my voice the next time I speak. "How could you do this to me?

To the other players? Do you realize how unfair you're being? I've passed up good-paying jobs with national corporations to make one last stab at being a professional baseball player. What baseball scout is going to come to watch perpetual exhibition games? You've ruined my chance of getting a professional contract.

"The worst thing is you've done it so subtly that I've enjoyed being deceived, I've enjoyed being part of your family, I've enjoyed thinking of how life might be if I stayed permanently in Grand Mound, worked with you year round. I was even thinking of how life might be if Tracy Ellen and I got together."

I'm shouting now. In frustration I bang my fist on the padded dashboard. Emmett eases the car to a stop. We are approaching a grove of trees, new, pale-green leaves aflutter in the morning breeze.

"It's not like that at all, Mike. The last thing we wanted to do was hurt you. I think deep down, you know that. You're a smart young man, and I like you a lot. I like you so much I'd be proud for you to stay in Grand Mound, to have you as a business partner, to have you as a son-in-law . . ."

"Stop it! This isn't the time to be selling Grand Mound to me, to be pimping your daughter. If things aren't the way I described, how are they? How do you see them?"

"Mike, there's a reason I drove out here. There's somebody else I want you to talk with. I realize you're disappointed, frustrated . . . but give us a few minutes of your time."

My teeth are clenched, my chest heaving in anger.

"And who might that mystery person be? Dilly Eastwick, recycler of nicknames? Suicide Walston, professional failure?

Maybe Tracy Ellen, armed with cherry pie and ice cream to seduce me into staying?"

We sit in silence for a few moments. I roll down my window and smell the tender odors of the earth, the greenness of the ankle-high corn. The sun is evaporating the dew, tendrils of steam rise from the nearby cornfield.

I can hear a car, Emmett is watching it in the rearview mirror, but I force myself not to turn around until it has pulled off the road behind us.

All my speculation has been wrong. It is the spotless, cream-colored Cadillac that sighs into silence as the ignition is turned off. Roger Cash unwinds from behind the wheel. He closes the door of the Cadillac carefully, brushing imaginary dirt off the door, and walks stiffly to Emmett's window. I let myself out of the passenger side and walk around the front of the Buick.

"I should have guessed," I say to Emmett, who is standing by the car. "If anyone is an expert at deception it's Mr. Cash here."

Emmett looks sharply at me. Doesn't he know of Roger Cash's past? Or, does he just not know that I know?

Roger leans carefully against the Cadillac. "Mike, I volunteered to talk to you when the time came. I pegged you as someone who'd need a lot of talking to. Besides, I've known you longest."

"You're smart, Mike. You're the only person who knows the secret of my career. I never got careless again."

I smile slightly in spite of myself. "You're not going to tell me this situation involves judging distances, are you?"

"Do you think it doesn't?" Roger asks, his voice gentle.

Roger Cash is dressed in a black leather jacket over a white turtleneck, a pair of pants the same color as his Cadillac, and black motorcycle boots. He looks as if he could play Fred Noonan, the handsome navigator who vanished forever into the blue Pacific with Amelia Earhart.

"Emmett," Roger says. "I'll drive this young man back to town after we have our chat. It may take a while, so would you open the ballpark for afternoon practice?" He tosses Emmett three keys on a ring.

Emmett looks worried.

"I'll do my best," Roger assures him.

"You take care, Mike. I'll see you later," says Emmett.

"Don't count on it," I say, but too softly for Emmett to hear.

He looks sad and a little bewildered as he eases the Buick into a U-turn and heads back toward Grand Mound.

TWENTY-FIVE

We wait until the drone of Emmett's car is beyond hearing before Roger speaks.

"Tell me what you think you know, Mike."

"Only that Grand Mound doesn't have a team in the Cornbelt League, that I've been wasting my time playing in a place big-league scouts don't know exists. I'm mad as hell. If I'd known I wasn't going to get a chance at pro ball I could be playing in Double A in Knoxville right now, or making serious money at IBM or some other corporation. All these people in Grand Mound are interested in doing is beefing up the population of the town and marrying off their daughters. Talk about weird."

"Those may appear to be the facts."

"I've already been through this with Emmett."

"Mike, what kind of a ballplayer were you in college?"

"What the hell's that got to do with the price of corn?"

"Just tell me the truth. What kind of a player were you in college?"

"I was pretty good. Dilly Eastwick published my statistics in the *Leader* and in the Greenshirts program. You must have read them. If you've become like everybody else in Grand Mound you probably memorized them."

"Statistics lie, Mike. Any real sports fan knows that. As Mark Twain said, there are lies, damn lies, and statistics. Your stats may have looked okay on paper, but what did you do when the pressure was on?"

It was like Roger was reading my mind. I could play wounded with Emmett. But Cash knew about distances and odds and the importance of performing in the clutch. He knew that one strikeout with the bases loaded is worth ten strikeouts with two out and nobody on.

"I . . . well . . ."

"What did you do when things got tough, Mike?"

"I choked. Dammit, I choked. Does it make you happy to hear me admit it? I'll say it again. I choked. Not that it has anything to do with my present situation. I haven't choked here. I'm playing like a pro. I liked it here so much that last week I turned down a chance to go to Double A in Knoxville. Did you know that? Oh, you probably did. Emmett's phone is probably tapped. And now I find out everything here is a fraud. I can see why *you* fit right in. I'm such a complete fool."

Roger didn't take the bait. I wanted to fight with him. Like Emmett, he simply smiled grimly when I insulted him.

"The year you had to impress the scouts, Mike, you choked.

Your stats in clutch situations have always been bad. We know that, and we understand."

"Wait a minute. Are you saying you recruited me *because* I've been known to choke? Are you saying everyone on the team is like me?"

"Including the manager."

I'd just thrown the statement out to be perverse. I can hardly believe it. A team of chokers. Suicide Walston. Of course, if anybody ever choked in the clutch, it'd be Suicide.

"Do the other players know?"

"About themselves? Yes. About what's going on in Grand Mound and why it's so special? Yes."

My mouth was hanging open.

"Are you aware how much razzing Emmett has taken from the boys down at the Doll House Café? The players even have a pool on the hour and day you'll twig."

Roger checks his watch. I can picture him announcing the exact time and date before practice, counting out bills into a grinning player's hand.

"After the first few days," he goes on, "after giving a new player time to acclimatize, we don't take a lot of pains to hide what's going down. You must have believed in the Tooth Fairy and the Easter Bunny for a long while, too."

"So, now I'm stupid as well as a choker?"

"Get the chip off your shoulder, Mike. Everybody wants to do what's best for *you*, to see that you do what's best for you."

"I didn't want to believe that anything out of the ordinary was going on here. Everything is so . . . perfect."

"You're right, it's perfect."

"But everyone else knows. How can I ever face them?"

"They've all gone through it. They've all survived."

"Dan Morgenstern left the team."

"He was a denier, Mike. Claimed he'd never choked in his life. Didn't believe a word we told him. He's better off back in New Jersey. Not happier, but better off."

"And Felix Rincon? He's a choker, too?"

"Why was he apprenticing as a plumber instead of playing professional baseball when we found him?"

"Is there something magical going on here?"

"Magical? No."

"A team that isn't a team?"

"Mike, look at what's been accomplished here in Grand Mound. The people who originally came up with the idea were years ahead of their time. They saw the future, Mike, saw that the small towns, not just in Iowa, but everywhere, were going to die, dry up and blow away like dandelion fluff.

"'How can we keep our town together?' they asked. 'How can we make Grand Mound prosper and grow, when all around America small towns are withering and dying? We can't stop our young people from going off to the cities, but maybe we could bring some young men here, baseball players, who, if we made life attractive for them, would stay with us, marry into the community, keep the faith, so to speak.'

"They tell me that at first the plan didn't work at all. Emmett and his friends saw baseball as the key to luring young men here, but Grand Mound didn't have a team in the Cornbelt League, and there was no possibility of getting one.

"At first talented players were recruited, but when they found out what was going on, what Emmett and the group really had in mind, that there was no team in the Cornbelt League, that they had been recruited simply to play inter-squad games for the entertainment of local fans, they scattered to the four winds like a flock of startled birds.

"Then someone, and I'm sure that someone was Dilly Eastwick, stumbled on the idea of recruiting players who had good solid statistics, but didn't come through in the clutch. There were hundreds of them out there, some of the Booster Club had been there themselves, pretty fair amateur ballplayers until the crunch came.

"In Grand Mound they gave those players a chance to play, to display their abilities in front of appreciative fans. Every player is assured by the manager, in private, soon after they arrive, that they've made the team. The players play well because they're not anxious, not worried about making a mistake. And play well they do, Mike. You're a prime example."

Roger Cash flashed his wide, winning smile at me.

"When they realize what's happening, don't some of them run off, too?"

"Oh, the first few years were pretty rough, they tell me, but you know, Mike, deep in his heart, every player who is a choker knows it. Every once in a while a Dan Morgenstern won't admit it; but for most, when they discover the truth about Grand Mound, it's such an immense relief to know the pressure's off, that they're grateful to Emmett and Dilly, and for the last few years, me, and make a real effort to fit into the community."

"But Tracy Ellen . . . how can I face her? She's known all along. She must have been laughing behind her hand at me all this time, her and that Neanderthal who drives that earthmoving machine he calls a truck."

"So you've been a little slow to catch on. You're not in Japan, Mike. Losing face isn't the be-all and end-all."

"I could take some kidding from the players, but not from Tracy Ellen. Besides I'm not . . ."

"Don't be a denier, Mike."

"I admit, I've choked in some situations. But I've also played well when the chips were down. God, if I can't perform in the clutch, what's going to happen to me when I'm in line for a promotion with some multinational corporation?"

"All the more reason to stay in Grand Mound. You'll never have to find out. You'll always be with people who love you and understand you."

"It's too pat, too perfect. It's like those few moments at sunset and dawn, when the light is perfect, the sky beautiful, and moviemakers shoot their love scenes."

"What if it were magic time all the time, Mike? I'm not saying it's possible, I'm just saying what if?"

Only a few hours before I had witnessed the wonder of dawn breaking over Grand Mound, the sky subtly changing color, the approaching sun a slash of molten metal across the eastern horizon.

"Look into the future, Mike," Roger went on. "Barring injury, you play second base for eight or ten years. About the time you retire from baseball Emmett will retire from his business and you'll take over. In a year or so, you'll marry Tracy Ellen. There will be children, a home, a happy life. One day you and Tracy Ellen will probably offer free board and room to a young ballplayer. You'll be inducted into the Grand Mound Booster Club. You'll be a director of the Grand Mound Greenshirts . . ."

"But if what you say is possible—and I'm not sure I believe that it is—I'll know exactly where my life is headed. There will be no surprises. I'm not sure I want to live like that."

"All fairway and no rough. Most people would grab at a chance like that, with both hands and their heart. It's called security, Mike. That's what you're being offered."

"But I didn't get a chance to prove myself in professional baseball. Will-power can overcome a lot of things, including choking in key situations."

"We're satisfied you can't overcome."

"Who the hell are you to be satisfied about what I can and can't do?"

"Don't do this, Mike."

"Come to think of it, what the hell are you doing living in Grand Mound, Roger? I'd have guessed you'd be selling water softeners, encyclopedias, or Florida swamp land."

"Feel free to speak your mind, Mike." Roger Cash laughs his deep, resonant laugh. "You don't beat around the bush do you? How long is it since we met? Six, seven years?"

"About that."

"You were what, seventeen? Well, I was thirty-six, so my life expectancy as a pitcher was pretty limited. But I kept pressing on. I didn't keep all my cash in the safe in the Caddy. There were a few deposit boxes scattered safely about the country. No pun intended.

"I didn't lose very often, Mike. But a couple of years after I met you, I drifted into Grand Mound and ended up at the Doll House Café recruiting a couple of boys to set up a game between Grand Mound High School with me pitching and the best local team, which turned out to be the Greenshirts, this odd semi-pro team that only played for their own amusement."

"So they whipped your ass, you lost everything, and you

had to stay in Grand Mound?"

"Not at all, although it always surprises me how much loose money there is in a small town. I happened to do an interview with Dilly Eastwick for the *Grand Mound Leader* that sort of disparaged small-town baseball. I didn't have a clue what was going on here, I was just looking for some way to pique interest in the game. So I said the reason I was able to win most of my games, even though I had only the local high-school team behind me was that most amateur teams choked when they faced professional pitching.

'Well, after that I had to wire away for more money to cover all the bets. Can you believe it! A town with a baseball club made up of professional chokers bet thousands of dollars that their team wouldn't choke."

"If they didn't beat you, what happened?"

"Don't hurry a good story, Mike. I did manage to have my usual advantage, but what I had to go through to get it made me consider retiring. Grand Mound had an old, arthritic groundskeeper who lived right in the equipment room at Fred Noonan Field. He didn't need much sleep, so when it came time for me to move the pitching rubber back six inches, I had to creep into the ballpark, and do all my groundskeeping practically lying down so as not to attract any attention, and being silent as a shadow, because in spite of his age that groundskeeper could hear the grass grow.

"The day of the game everything went as expected. We scored four runs in the first, and one more in the second, and I went into the seventh with a 5-3 lead. The second pitch to the second batter I faced was a fastball out of the strike zone. But as I let it go something popped in my shoulder. The noise was so loud that I thought the batter had fouled the pitch off. Then the pain hit me. My arm just hung at my side.

"My career was over, but there were more immediate problems—there was no provision for injury in the contract. It was all verbal: the Greenshirts against the high-school team with me pitching, but nothing about what should happen if I couldn't pitch.

"I could try to employ the five-inning rule. Saying that since five innings had been played the game was complete—a 5-3 victory for us.

"They could counter, saying the only thing that could stop a game was weather or an act of war. They could also say that since I was unable to continue the game had to be defaulted.

"I thought that the most likely scenario. I decided I'd willingly forfeit the game, but since it wasn't a complete game I'd suggest the bets be voided and all money returned.

"Turned out I didn't have to worry, Mike. While Doctor Greenspan was appraising my arm, Dilly and Emmett were telling me that since I couldn't continue, something that appeared pretty obvious, all bets were off because they didn't want to take advantage of my injury.

"Doctor Greenspan X-rayed me and wanted to put me in the nearest hospital for a day or two, but I had to beg off. These people were killing me with kindness, and I had a ball field to repair. It was the first time I ever felt guilty, Mike. Here I'd been taking advantage of these people, and now that I was injured they were falling all over themselves to be nice to me.

"I was rooming at the home of a young widow whose husband had been killed in Vietnam. I am never averse to female company, so we had spent a delightful week together.

"Mike, if you think I didn't have a difficult time getting out of that house in the middle of the night, you just think again. My shoulder was so sore it felt, in spite of the medication Dr. Greenspan had given me, like a pistol was being fired into it at about thirty-second intervals. And Janet, the woman I was boarding with, was so happy to have someone to nurse that she hardly left me alone for a minute.

"But I escaped and got to the ballpark, tippy-toed out of the house like a burglar. Three in the morning and there I am with garden tools on my left shoulder and wondering how I can repair the mound with only one arm, and in so much pain I saw red stars every time I bent over even slightly.

"Then, Mike, I discovered a most remarkable thing. I had to measure from the plate to the mound to establish where to set the rubber so the distance between the two would be exactly sixty feet six inches. I had to place a rock on the end of my tape on the plate and then pull the tape awkwardly until I got it to the mound.

"I measured and measured, but the distance between the plate and the rubber was already sixty feet six inches.

"I never did find out when the rubber had been replaced. Was it before or after the game? Did we score legitimate runs in the first and second inning? Or was my sinister groundskeeping repaired after the game was over? I've never found out.

"By the time my shoulder healed enough for me to think of looking for work, I was seriously involved with Janet. All the mornings of my convalescence were spent in the Doll House Café, afternoons and evenings with Janet at the ballpark. I'd checked my finances and decided I had enough money to live comfortably if I held a part-time job of some sort, something that would just earn me grocery money. The day Janet and I announced our marriage plans the old groundskeeper announced his retirement, and Dilly and Emmett and a delegation of townspeople offered me the job at Fred Noonan Field.

"Mike, I have never been happier. I have two sons, and a baby girl just two months old. My oldest's going to be a left-handed pitcher, and, who knows, maybe when the time comes I'll teach him all about distances.

"Mike, trust me. We in Grand Mound have done our homework: we've studied the distances, we've done our groundskeeping . . ."

"Meaning what?"

"Emmett probably hasn't mentioned that the whole family scouted you—Emmett, Marge, and Tracy Ellen."

"Tracy Ellen?"

"The three of them flew down to Baton Rouge and watched you play a half-dozen games. They even sat next to you in a restaurant called the Blue . . . Blue . . . something."

"The Blue Parrot."

"Right. You never noticed them, of course. You were with a girl, and another couple: you ordered roast beef, iced tea, and cherry pie à la mode."

"Tracy Ellen was there?"

"You were her choice for second base."

"Then what about Shag Wilson? Him and his goddamned earth-moving truck?"

"Shag Wilson's a lot nicer boy than Emmett's let on. If you check you'll find that Emmett gives him a whopping discount on his insurance . . ."

"That's worse than devious."

"Mike, are you happy? Have you been happy here in Grand Mound these past few weeks?"

"Yes, I've been happy."

"Then I rest my case. Grand Mound rests its case. You've got information to process, Mike. Skip practice this afternoon, the game tonight if you want. Sleep on it. If you honestly think you can catch on with a professional ball club, and if your heart's set on giving it a try, no one in Grand Mound will stand in your way."

"I don't believe you," I said, moving away from the white Cadillac, which was no longer the antiseptic vehicle I had known. The signs of family life bloomed like small desecrations on the upholstery, a spill here, a crease there: toys, towels, a pair of tiny multi-colored bathing trunks on the back seat, a teething ring hanging from the knob of the cigarette lighter.

"Get in," said Roger. "I'll drive you back to town."

"No. I can't face the people of Grand Mound."

What I meant was I couldn't face Tracy Ellen. I can't stand the thought of someone I may be in love with laughing at my gullibility, my naïvety. I could picture Tracy Ellen and Shag Wilson howling at my stupidity, wondering when I'd catch on.

"They tell me you're the best second-base man who's ever played at Fred Noonan Field."

"Yeah, and who told you that? The ever-reliable Dilly Eastwick? I'll let you know where to send my belongings," I said walking away from the Cadillac.

"This is a secondary road, Mike. What have we seen, two cars since we've been out here?"

"I can walk."

"I'll give you a ride."

211

"You've done enough for me already."

"Suit yourself, Mike. I'll watch for your stats in *Baseball America*."

"You do that," I said, turning my back.

TWENTY-SIX

Cedar Rapids Airport.

I didn't look back even once until I was sure Roger Cash and the Cadillac would be well out of sight. It was approaching noon. The sky was a cloudless blue from horizon to horizon. The only sounds were the trembling of leaves on a few aspens alongside the road. A hawk circled silently; in fact, I was unaware of it until its shadow crossed the highway just a few feet in front of me. The eeriest of feelings. I could smell the corn growing.

I walked down the highway listening for the sounds of a vehicle approaching from behind me so I could begin hitchhiking. I turned and studied each approaching vehicle closely. I kept expecting to be picked up by Emmett, or Dilly Eastwick, or even one of my teammates. I fantasized that there was no way I could leave Grand Mound. Every driver would recognize me as a baseball player trying to escape and attempt to return me, by force if necessary, to Fred Noonan Field.

Eventually I got a five-mile ride with a tanker driver who knew nothing and cared nothing about the Cornbelt League or Grand Mound, or whether I was going to find personal happiness, or make it as a professional baseball player. I got two more short rides, so short I was still looking over my shoulder prepared to run if I spotted someone from Grand Mound, when, at a pay phone in a motel parking lot on the outskirts of a nameless town, I placed a collect call to Justin Birdsong.

There was a very long pause while Justin considered the information the operator gave him, evaluating the cost of the call against what he had to offer me.

"I'll accept the charges," Justin Birdsong said.

"Any chance that the Knoxville position is still open?"

"What happened to Grand Mound? A week ago you were going to stay there forever."

"Everything fell apart in Grand Mound. They lied about everything. Don't ever send anyone else there. They don't have a team in the Cornbelt League, all they do is play inter-squad games. But my play was real good. I was batting .333 and fielding like a Hoover."

"Well, you're in luck. They still need somebody with experience in Knoxville, almost every second-base man and utility infielder in their organization is injured, and while they have a couple of hot shots in Class A ball, they don't want to advance them too quickly."

"So I've got it?"

"Are you still in Grand Mound?"

"No. I'm hitchhiking."

"Well, give me a number where I can wire the plane fare. Knoxville's at home; you can probably be their starting secondbase man tomorrow night."

Once I got to the Cedar Rapids Airport, I collected the money, got a handful of quarters and called Roger Cash's house. I figured he'd be at the ballpark. There were children shrieking in the background when his wife answered. I'd seen Janet Cash at the ballpark many evenings, a short, dark-complexioned, very beautiful woman, who often nursed her baby daughter while her twin sons pulled at her sleeves for attention. I told her where Roger could send my belongings, then sat back to wait for my plane. I kept one eye on the main door to the airport lounge in case a delegation from Grand Mound might come in search of me.

But instead of thinking about what lay ahead of me in Knoxville, as I waited in the almost empty airport for my flight out of Iowa, I wondered about Tracy Ellen. I wondered if, late at night, she and Shag Wilson made love in the fur-lined cab of his wheeled monstrosity, maybe parked in some aspen grove beyond the river; or maybe I had been completely fooled and she was like other girls I dated, and they did it parked in the loading zone in front of the Wheatland Theater on the main street.

Was I doing the right thing?

It had to be the right thing. I was getting my big chance, my last chance to be a professional ballplayer. Baseball was what counted. The Tracy Ellens of my life would have to wait at least until the end of the season.

TWENTY-SEVEN

Knoxville, Tennessee. It's been three weeks since I became the starting second-base man.

I think we played a better class of baseball in Grand Mound, more consistent at least. Consistency is what baseball is all about, the main difference between major leaguers and minor leaguers. A major leaguer will make a certain play successfully 499 out of 500 times, while a minor leaguer will make ten more errors, and get only a few seasons in the minors.

Here in Knoxville there are too many 10-9 and 14-7 games. At this level of baseball, hitting outranks pitching. Each team seems to have one starter with major-league potential, and one reliever who, they hope, will be an adequate closer someday. The rest of their pitching is mediocre at best.

The evenings seem to go on forever. The fans, who don't turn out in large numbers, drift away in the late innings. Our games are usually over three hours long, sometimes three and a half without extra innings, too long to bear down the whole time.

I decided I was going to play just as I had in Grand Mound, as if I was the permanent second-base man, but imagination is one thing, being a starting second-base man in Double A baseball is another.

My problem is that things are not going well for me here in Knoxville. I wake up with that white-hot burning at the base of my breastbone. Nerves? Ulcer? Whatever it is, it makes my life miserable. My pockets are full of antacid tablets. I share a tacky one-bedroom apartment with a black outfielder named Parton Jones. It's littered with Maalox bottles. It's surprising how quickly I became accustomed to living with the Powells, the home cooking, the clean room, being with people who genuinely cared. I miss those wonderful meals, I even miss Emmett's corny jokes, and I miss Tracy Ellen most of all.

I wake up in the middle of the night, my heart thudding, my mouth dry, my insides churning. I've been having my trapped dreams again. On a double-play ball to shortstop I try to cover second base, but my feet are rooted to the ground. The soft toss goes directly to the empty bag and rolls on into the outfield as the runners careen around the bases. Only when the play is over are my feet released. I can hear the booing of the fans, feel the derision of my teammates.

I have not had one minute's fun since I came here. All right, a ballplayer struggling toward a major-league career is not supposed to have fun, but when I look in the mirror all I can see is the dark circles under my haunted eyes.

"You don't need to use charcoal on high-skied, sunny days," one of the players needled me a few days ago. I see the crease between my brows deep as if it were gouged out, and getting deeper.

I'm hanging on. That's the best that can be said for me. I'm batting .270, which in Double A is satisfactory, nothing more. I've never been more than an adequate fielder; my range is not spectacular, but I can get by if I concentrate. Most of my career I've been able to concentrate. To bear down.

"Concentrate, anticipate, levitate," one of my college coaches used to enthuse, claiming that if we mastered the first two, the third would take care of itself.

But I haven't been concentrating, haven't been anticipating, which makes levitating the most wishful of thinking.

Last weekend, Dad and Peggy McNee flew down to watch me play. They described it as a pre-honeymoon holiday. Dad is living in Grand Mound, working for the lumberyard. He and Peggy are getting married the Labor Day weekend. As hard as it is for me to imagine, it's going to be a big wedding.

"A wedding is a community event," Peggy McNee said. "People expect a bit of a show."

Dad and she grinned amiably.

"Isn't love grand," I wanted to say, but why antagonize anyone? In truth, love *is* grand. And Dad looks happier than I ever remember.

"We're each going to have four attendants," Dad said.

Four attendants!

"Emmett Powell, Roger Cash, you, and Byron will be mine. You'll have to rent a tuxedo. Mine's going to be powder blue. Peggy's already picked it out, and taken all my measurements."

"I imagine you two had the most fun measuring the inseam," I'm tempted to say, but of course I don't.

Am I jealous of my dad's happiness? If I was going to pick out a new wife for him, I'd have a difficult time finding some nicer than Peggy McNee. So what's my problem?

Dad could tell right away that something was wrong. He and Peggy took me out to dinner at a fancy restaurant left over from the Knoxville World's Fair.

"I don't hear you breaking down a lot of statistics for me. According to last week's *Baseball America* you're not doing too bad. So what's the problem, Mike?"

"I'm not doing too bad. I'm just not doing too good. It's the same problem I had my last year at LSU. I'm not holding up under the pressure. And my stomach is killing me."

I honestly expected a pep talk from Dad. I was all set for one, even expecting it to perk me up, at least temporarily.

Instead, Dad said, "Come back to Grand Mound, Son. Everybody misses you."

Peggy nodded her agreement.

"How can I?" I said. "I feel like I burned a lot of bridges behind me. You're family. You can forgive me."

"Everybody misses you," Dad repeated.

I'd never known him to lie; still, I wasn't sure I could believe him.

In the seventh inning of Saturday night's game my worst fear materialized. The opposition had a runner on first. We were in a one-run game so they were probably going to sacrifice the runner to second.

Earlier, with a runner on first and likely to steal, the shortstop and I exchanged signals, establishing who would cover the bag in the event of a steal. But when the runner took off neither of us covered the bag. The fans didn't know who to blame, but I knew. And the shortstop knew. And the manager knew.

When the sacrifice bunt came in the seventh, laid down perfectly along the first-base line, the pitcher and first-base man charged the ball. The first-base man fielded it, and, having no play at second, turned to toss it to me at first. But I had not even moved. Just like in my dream, my feet had been bolted to the earth. And while everyone else was in motion about the field, including the umpires getting in position to make the necessary calls, I stood like a statue, watching everything in slow motion.

Management wasn't surprised when I told them I was retiring, because, so I said, "Three M has made me an offer I can't refuse."

I left my rent paid to the end of the month, and arranged for my final pay check to be sent to my dad in care of Peggy McNee. I only had enough for bus fare to Peoria. And I wasn't about to beg from anybody. My trusty thumb moved me along in short hops. At the first truck-stop coffee shop inside Iowa I look at the small, round woman with lank black hair who stops in front of me to take my order.

"Do you know the perfect name for a waitress?" I ask.

My luck ran out just after midnight.

Twenty miles out of Grand Mound. At night the traffic on secondary highways in rural Iowa all but disappears, and the few vehicles that passed, their headlights picking me up at the last moment, were not inclined to stop for a tall, dark figure, elongated even more by the sudden slash of headlights, a duffel bag over its shoulder like a deformity.

I could have lain down in a ditch until morning. The sky is clear, the humidity high, the air thick and sweet with the scents of new growth. Instead, I plod along, followed by the three-quarter moon, fat and butter-colored, seeming to make the night even warmer. I can hear the scurrying of tiny, nocturnal animals. An owl wafts silently from a roadside tree, glides over a field, makes a sudden knife-like dive, skimming the earth, rising with something unlucky clutched in its talons.

I plunged quarters into a drink machine at a dark, silent service station, the chatter of the coins, the can of sweet liquid crashing down like a rock slide, booming through the still night.

As I plod along the twisting asphalt, fields of knee-high corn on either side of me, I think of all that has happened to me since the fateful spring day when Justin Birdsong offered me a baseball job in Grand Mound, Iowa.

I think of the players: Dan Morgenstern, who is gone, I assume for good; Dan who couldn't face the fact that he choked in the clutch. Crease Fowler who, unlike the rest of us, never wanted to play professionally, always wanted to play for fun. He is the one who fits in best. He is totally happy to be given the opportunity to carve a niche for himself in Grand Mound. He's fallen in love, and it hasn't done him irreparable damage. I remember him joking the last time I saw him: "Barbara's really great at showing me a good time. I take her out to dinner and she says, 'Look at that couple, they're having a good time," and, 'Look at that family, they're having a good time.'"

And, finally, Barry McMartin, who will soon be gone headed for a couple of weeks of conditioning in Triple A and then to the Bigs, where in a year or two he'll be getting a three-or-four-million-dollar-a-year contract.

Dad told me last weekend McMartin may well be an off-season resident of Grand Mound. "It's the talk of the town in more ways than one," Dad said. "It must have been the day after you left, the Millers' son Malcolm came home from college. It took Barry about twelve hours to admit to Malcolm that he was gay."

"The Millers and Emmett and the Grand Mound Booster Club were keeping Barry in town, under wraps, until Malcolm Miller got home? They knew what was going to happen?"

"They suspected. Apparently Malcolm's always been a gentle, understanding boy, and upfront about being gay. Everyone involved felt Barry would be perfect for him."

When I reached Grand Mound, my way was still lit by moonlight. As I walked through the town, the purring of a streetlight the only sound, the stars were so close I felt if I jumped just a little I could catch a handful of them to bring to Tracy Ellen. The first hint of light was appearing in the eastern sky as I lowered my duffel bag onto the grass in Emmett's front yard, and made my way to a spot below Tracy Ellen's window.

I plinked stone chips off her window.

Nothing.

I plinked some more.

Across the yard, I heard a window on the second floor of Peggy McNee's house open. My dad's large head appeared, his blue-black hair looking like he'd just come out of a windstorm.

"Welcome home, Son," he boomed.

"You're not mad I woke you?" I whispered.

"Shall I phone Tracy Ellen and let her know you're out here?"

"Shhhh!"

Tracy Ellen's window slid open.

As I turned toward her, my dad disappeared inside Peggy's house.

"Mike?"

"Will you come down, Tracy Ellen? I need to talk with you."

"The last time you ran away."

"I won't do that again. I promise."

She disappeared from the window.

I was sitting on the front step when she came out. Her eyes still held the surprise of being wakened. She was wearing jeans and a heavy Greenshirts sweat shirt. One of her sneakers was untied.

"Let me," I said, pointing.

"Did it ever occur to you to wait until a decent time of day?" she asked as I tied her shoe laces.

"Not even once," I said. "I've walked all night to get here."

I took her hand and we headed toward the town.

"You're going to stay this time? You're not mad at us? At me?"

"I was never mad at you, Tracy Ellen. I'm sorry I ran away."

"You were just too trusting, Mike."

"How can I stay mad? How can I be angry at people like

your dad, like Roger Cash, even at Dilly Eastwick? They genuinely mean well. They seem to know me better than I know myself. There's only one person who can make me leave again, and that's you."

"I wanted to go after you. Dad practically had to tie me down. He and Roger convinced me you had to try your hand at being a pro."

"What if I'd been successful? What if I hadn't come back? Would you and your family have gone on another scouting trip, lined up another baseball-playing sweetheart for yourself?"

"I'd have come looking for you."

I took her in my arms then, tentatively at first, for she was light and fragile against me, but there was a delightful tenacity to the way she held the hair at the back of my neck as she pressed her mouth into mine.

As the enormous sun poked itself above the horizon like a dark-edged sunflower, turning the eastern skyline flame-colored, I could see in the opposite direction the moon, pale as ice, descending, a fleeting touch of pink from the sky making it dainty as a floating ballet slipper.

Heading back to the house, Tracy Ellen's hand held tightly in mine, I thought of Roger Cash. He had been right; what had happened was all about distances, about the distances between people, about the distances between trust and love, the distances between truth and reality.

We tiptoed up the front walk and sat on the swing, Tracy Ellen with her legs curled under her, an arm around me, her head on my shoulder, her pale hair turned fiery by the rising sun.

"The fourth of July is coming up," Tracy Ellen said.

"The Greenshirts play a doubleheader," I said.

"Fireworks afterward."

"Fireworks are only fun if you can watch them with someone you love, someone you can hold hands with, and maybe kiss once or twice."

"When did you know you were going to come back to Grand Mound?"

"I think, deep down, I've known all along. There's something about the way you wave goodbye in the mornings, as if you really mean it, as if you'll truly miss me, that just breaks my heart."

About the Author

W. P. (Bill) Kinsella is the author of some twenty-four books and more than two hundred stories. He is best known for his baseball fiction: *The Thrill of the Grass*; *Go the Distance*; *The Iowa Baseball Confederacy*; *The Dixon Cornbelt League*; *Box Socials*; and *Shoeless Joe*, his multi-award-winning novel that became the classic movie *Field of Dreams*, nominated for three Academy Awards, including Best Picture.

Kinsella's other books include *Dance Me Outside* (also made into a feature film); *Scars*; *Born Indian*; *The Moccasin Telegraph*; *The Fencepost Chronicles*; *The Miss Hobbema Pageant*; and *Red Wolf, Red Wolf*, from which the story "Lieberman in Love" was adapted for the screen and went on to win an Academy Award for Best Short Feature. His most recent novel, *If Wishes Were Horses*, has been optioned by Fox 2000.

Magic Time has been optioned by the producers of *The Natural*.

Photograph copyright by Bridget Turner Kinsella